Wendell Ford

JOB

THE POWER OF
NEGATIVE THINKING

RELIANT
PUBLISHING
A DIVISION OF REDEMPTION PRESS

Published by Reliant Publishing, an imprint of Redemption Press, PO Box 427, Enumclaw, WA 98022.

Toll-Free (844) 2REDEEM (273-3336)

Redemption Press is honored to present this title in partnership with the author. The views expressed or implied in this work are those of the author. Redemption Press provides our imprint seal representing design excellence, creative content, and high-quality production.

ISBN 13: 978-1-64645-303-0 (Paperback)
978-1-64645-305-4 (ePub)
978-1-64645-304-7 (Mobi)

Library of Congress Catalog Card Number: 2020921764

Also by the author

Humor in the Writings of Paul
Genesis 1, 2, 3, and Beyond

Contents

Preface

A real writer learns from earlier writers the way a boy learns from an apple orchard—by stealing what he has a taste for, and can carry off.

—Archibald MacLeish

In Proverbs 23:7 in the KJV appears the phrase: "As a man thinketh in his heart, so is he." It has been taken out of context ever since and used as an axiom; almost everyone has heard it. Newer translations phrase it quite differently; however, the basic idea does appear throughout the Bible. Modern psychology affirms that our thoughts can have great influence on us. Behavioral and motivational psychologists recognize how important our attitudes and thoughts are in determining who we are. Norman Vincent Peale wrote *The Power of Positive Thinking* (1952), and Dennis Waitley wrote *The Psychology of Winning* (1979)—both books stress the importance of how we think about things. The well-known children's story *The Little Engine That Could* teaches a positive motivational lesson. Medical research suggests that negative thinking in old age contributes to Alzheimer's disease. In the *Star Wars* movies, Yoda points out to Luke Skywalker, "You do or don't do; there is no try."

Generally the Book of Job is used as an example of integrity, loyalty, and patience; however, if we consider it closely, we see a lot of negative thinking and how it steers the progression of the discussions. Due to the poetic structure of the book (chapters 3–41), it is easy to get bogged down and not follow through with a train of thought and seems very repetitive because it is. Job's three friends have an opinion and stick to it, but Job does have some development in his opinion. To maintain continuity, one needs to consider the dialogue (chapters 3–27) as a whole and to read in one sitting. Then it is possible to follow certain themes though the book. In this book we will trace some of these themes and notice the negative thinking and its impact.

Job is probably one of the more neglected books in the Bible. There are many reasons for this. It is tucked away between the books of history which are easy to read and the other books of poetry which have an appeal and comfort. Job is also poetry, of course, but of a different nature which makes it more difficult to read. Hebrew poetry consists not in the rhyming of sound but the rhyming of the thought. Usually it is a couplet of lines as in Psalms and Proverbs, yet in Job this is carried on for many lines with the crux of the thought being repeated in many different ways. Thus one may think that there is not progression in the text. Actually a closer reading shows a development of ideas as the book proceeds.

Another hindrance is the sudden shift from the easy-to-read prose of the first two chapters to the poetry of the next thirty-nine chapters. There is also a dramatic change in the subject, which can catch one by surprise. It is said that the Hebrew is the most difficult to read in the Bible. Many of the Hebrew words are rare, some used only once and not found in other literature. For those of us who have to rely on translations into English, we find many variations. Translating is never exact because there is never an exact equivalence between words of different languages. In spite of all of this, Job has caught the attention of biblical scholars and serious readers. They have discovered that Job is much more profound than a casual approach to the book may indicate. The result is that a surprising number of books have been written about Job. The authors extract a lot of different teachings from Job which is indicative of the great depth of the book. The story of Job has also inspired artists as they interpret many scenes from the book.

A person who is interested in studying Job can find a wide variety of approaches to the study. There are the classic commentaries that take it a verse, or even a word, at a time and do an in depth analysis of it. I find these hard to read straight through and gain much overall understanding, but they are good for resolving a particular point. Other authors use it for devotional use or for inspirational sessions. Some take a particular theme and develop it from what they find in Job. This illustrates the depth and profoundness of the book and illustrates how difficult it is to narrow down a selection of books that would serve one's interests. Computer searches are complicated by the fact that "job" to most means "occupation" and a lot of matches reference that meaning. Using "Bible" or "biblical" in the search parameters helps. Very few authors try to gain any historical perspective from the Book of Job. At this time perhaps all of the perspectives possible have been explored by some author or perhaps not.

As many of the books written about Job are rare, out of print, or otherwise hard to find, it is hard to learn all of the perspectives or even if they exist. I have read some of these over the years, but certainly only a small sample, and so am not familiar with every view. If one has a deep interest in Job, it behooves them to read several. The views, insights, and conclusions will be vastly different; even conflicting at times. This does not mean that any one is more correct or enlightening than another; it means only that the author had a particular perspective at the time of writing. A perspective that may be dismissed now may prove to be more relevant later because our life's circumstances have changed. The book that was the breakthrough in 1963 for me to finally gain a real appreciation for Job is Reference 1. (Unfortunately many, many years ago I loaned my copy to someone who never returned it, so have had to rely on notes I had taken and what I can remember. I have forgotten to whom it was I loaned it.) I am not sure how available it is now, so I will refer to some of the thoughts from it that I think ought to be preserved and recognized. I have taught Job a few times to adult Bible classes and was helped most by that book. Every class I taught was a little different because each time I discovered something new or saw something from a different angle. Sometimes I even changed or modified my ideas, perhaps because my situation or experiences had changed, or because something in the world culture had changed, or because I had a different audience with different needs.

That there is a universal appeal in the story of Job is seen in how often it is referred to and elements of the theme in it are used by others. A play (named simply *J. B.*), written in free verse and first performed in 1958, by Archibald MacLeish, is a telling of the Book of Job. It won a Pulitzer Prize. Herman Melville has many allusions to Job in his novel *Moby Dick*. He even has the owner of Captain Ahab's ship as Captain Bildad, a pious, hard-hearted Quaker. The novel ends with "And only I am escaped alone to tell thee." In 1818 William Blake created watercolors depicting his interpretation of the Book of Job. A couple of years later he made engravings of them. Many people think that the 1900 children's fantasy by L. Frank Baum, *The Wizard of Oz,* was influenced by the Book of Job noting the similarity between the land Oz and the land of Uz. Whether real or not, intended or not, many people see allusions to Job in other literary works. Doubtless many other stories will seem to be related to Job because people feel they are in the same predicament of being falsely accused. There are cases of some-one having their previous criminal conviction overturned many years later because of new evidence. It matters not whether they did other wrongs in the past but whether they were being punished for the wrong reason. In the Book of Job we are told that he is innocent of any wrong doing; for others it is only necessary that they feel they have done no wrong to experience the same outrage and despair. There is a stigma, deserved or not, attached to anyone who has ever been accused. Popular opinion can forever haunt the victim who is then shunned and ostracized by the community. Self-righteous and proper people avoid them. An example is the treatment of the homeless, a condition not duplicated since the Great Depression.

A very small sample of the kinds of approaches that have been used to characterize the Book of Job can be seen by the titles of books written about it. The first three references attest to that. References one through four are a cross-section of the treatment of the Book of Job. They span a period of writing of sixty-plus years. Carstensen focuses on Job defending his honor, as the title of the book implies. He makes use of ancient Greek literature to illustrate the prevalence of thought in the first millennium BC. His book is very readable yet offers profound insights. Where he has emphasized *honor*, I would probably consider *integrity* more. Safire, who was a political columnist for the *New York Times*, applied the Book of Job to the politics of time of his writing (1992). His intimate involvement with many of the significant historical politicians and events for about three decades provides very interesting reading for anyone interested in that era. He was an avid student of Job and collected a large number of books. Morgan (1863–1945) was pastor of Westminster Chapel in London, taught fourteen years at Biola College (now Biola University) in the Los Angeles area, and was a very prolific writer of over one hundred works. His book is of an inspirational or devotional nature. Walton is a professor of Old Testament at Wheaton College. His book is a considerable work (450-plus pages) that covers technical details through application (as the name of the series would imply). The books by Safire and Walton contain extensive bibliographies that don't duplicate any titles. This indicates that the message of Job can strike different people in different ways. It is not that anyone has a better insight than another but rather that Job is inclusive enough to cover a wide variety of one's inner struggles. Naturally all of the books will have the same basic details concerning the background and origin of the book. It is, after all, a part of the Bible. For the sheer number of volumes written about Job duplication happens. It may be impossible to present ideas that have not appeared before. What I am presenting is simply another dimension to an already mega-dimensional universe. Each reading of Job can evoke different thoughts. One should not expect to discover in Job a solution to a current problem, but perhaps one can expect that the insight gained will have relevance at a later time. The value of Job is not a "go to" source for solutions to problems but is a source of building understanding and strength. A one time reading is not sufficient. One needs to return to Job on occasion simply for the pleasure of reading it. I find humor in it as well as deep, soul searching insights because it deals with the inward trials and foibles of all of us. Job is a platform for exposing the fears, anxieties, and questions we encounter as we go through life. At the beginning of each chapter I will have a quote by Archibald MacLeish that may have some insight to the chapter, is interesting for other reasons, or simply because I liked them. These were obtained by doing a web search on "Archibald MacLeish Quotes." I received quite a number of hits and these quotes were taken from various ones. A lot of the quotes were present on a lot of web sites. Most did not give an exact source of the quote (much to my frustration) but are probably mostly from the play *J. B.* A typical site is: www.azquotes.com/author/9220-Arichibald-Macleish.

Because we are humans we are curious and want to know why things are the way they are. We want to know why things happen and the meaning behind them. Those who think more deeply want to know more about their existence, why we are here, and what is the meaning of life. Philosophers have dealt with such questions almost since the beginning of recorded history. People want to think there is something more to their lives than merely to exist. This is a basic difference between humans and other animals. It is hard to focus on such thoughts when life seems to be going well and is full of contentment. On the other hand when everything seems to be going wrong, especially if there is pain and suffering, then one tends to consider what life is all about. Feelings are aroused that were once latent and not worthy of consideration. We are social creatures and want the approval and empathy of others. If these are denied because of conditions for which we don't understand or don't know their source, then the sting of rejection greatly increases our woes. To discover that there are others in a similar situation both comforts and discourages us. If our fight is shared by others, it becomes easier to battle our own problems. Our arguments against our condition achieve a higher aim and our defense is strengthened. We are not alone in being abandoned and victimized.

In dealing with hypothetical problems (or even someone else's), it is easier to provide solutions and propose actions, if we don't have to implement them for our own comfort. Problems brought on people by themselves are apparent and, hence, the solution is apparent. No one feels they deserve the bad things that happen to them (they may have a different opinion about the good things). Religious people may reason that they should be exempt from many of the troubles experienced by the non-religious. Suffering ennobles only if it happens to someone else. Desperation can lead to actions and words that otherwise would never have been considered. Sources of relief are grasped that have little or no connection to the situation or reality.

People have often been referred to the Book of Job to find solace for their pain and anguish. To read the first two chapters and the last part of chapter 42, a story is constructed that implies that if one is patient enough, everything will turn out all right in the end. Delving deeper into the bulk of the book reveals a more complicated story. Issues are explored and questions asked that never occurred before. The basic question of "Why?" is never answered. Patience and how to obtain it are not addressed. If anything, the lack of patience is displayed and the frustration that accompanies it. Surprisingly, the way to a positive attitude is not shown, and a lot of negativity is expressed. In my last foray through the Book of Job, I discovered that negative thinking plays a key role in Job's life and also in our own lives. As I go through Job, I will take note of negative ideas expounded and how they shape the flow of the book and how we can use the power of negative thinking to shape our own lives.

CHAPTER 1

The Background

There is only one thing more painful than learning from experience and that is not learning from experience.
—Archibald MacLeish

The Book of Job is a bit of an enigma as a part of the Bible. At forty-two chapters, it is a significant work. As a work of poetry, Job introduces the Bible reader to other books of poetry that follow it. Understanding any book of the Bible is greatly aided by knowing as much about it as possible; the further from our own time the book is, the more important this becomes and may be harder to do. Background is asking a number of questions about the book. Who wrote it? Why was it written? Who was the original intended audience? When was it written and when did the events take place? Where was the physical location? What was the political climate? What is its relation to the rest of the Bible? How was it received? Why is it in the Bible? What is its relevance to us?

For the Book of Job, the answer to very few of the questions is provided; not in the book itself, not in other Scripture, not in literature contemporary with Job. There are, of course, clues, but very few. Thus the way is open for a lot of speculation. Ultimately the value of the book is what it contains and how it speaks to us; for that, the answers to the questions above are immaterial. Because we are so curious, the speculation about the questions helps to satisfy that curiosity, even if no definitive answers are forthcoming.

The Bible is one continuous story, from the very beginning of time to the prophecy of the end of time, of God's dealings with humans. It begins with their first disobedience and continues to their final salvation. As such it describes only those events and people significant to that story. There would obviously be much going on in the world that was not recorded in the Bible; there are a lot of details left out of the story that is told. The Book of Job is the only book in the Bible that is not directly telling part of the story (Ecclesiastes, Jonah, and Song of Solomon may be on the fringe). Its purpose may be more to clarify part of the nature of God and His relationship with humans and deals with issues that are much deeper than could fit into the telling of the story.

Because of the uniqueness of the book, at least four ideas have been suggested as to its nature. The first is that it is a history of real events involving real people. This would be the initial inclination because the Bible consists of real stories of real people. However, there is a connection and a continuity to all of those stories that make them part of a larger story. Job is isolated. There is no connection to other events or other people directly, but a few clues are present. These will be discussed later when we consider location of the events in the book. Job is mentioned twice, once in the Old Testament (Ezekiel 14:14 as righteous) and once in the New Testament (James 5:11 as steadfast). And that is all; nothing else about his character or life is discussed. The poetry in the book is considered by many to be the finest and most profound of all Hebrew poetry. How could a person in Job's condition spontaneous produce such poetry?

This leads to the second idea that the book is a parable. There is immediate objection to this; that the Bible would not include something that was not absolute truth. This view ignores the fact that parables are very much a part of biblical teaching and secular teaching of the times. The fables of Aesop were a popular teaching tool in the first millennium BC. They were obviously only stories because several used animals as the characters. To someone who does not think the Old Testament uses such a device, one only has to refer to 2 Samuel 12:1–6 where Nathan tells David about a rich man taking a lamb from a poor man. When David is incensed at the action of the rich man, Nathan says to David, "You are the man." So this is a parable; why might others not exist in the Old Testament (Psalms 78:2)? Jesus used many parables in his teaching and they are plainly recognized as such (Matthew 13:10–16).

The third possibility is that it was a dramatic play performed for moral teaching. Several Greek plays exist from the first millennium BC so the device was well known. However, there is no known example in the Bible.

The fourth possibility would be that it was an epic poem. That was a popular contemporary literature form, especially with the Greeks of the time. The Psalms are this form although none of them actually comprise a story. The great teachings of the book are in no way dependent on which type of literature Job is. None of the points in the Book of Job are tied to the nature of the story. It's the story itself and the issues raised in the discussion that are important. Perhaps it is a combination of all of them. Maybe there were real people who experienced the real events; the story was passed down in the oral lore so much that it achieved parable status; someone finally decided it needed to be preserved in written form as an epic poem which later was performed as a drama. Choose whatever form satisfies you the most and let the book speak to you.

There are three dates that can be considered in relation to the Book of Job. Part of the genius of Job is that it was written such that none of the dates affect the content. The first date is "When did the events take place?" The second is "When was the story composed?" The third is "When was the book written down?" There are no definitive answers to these, but there are a few clues from which inferences and educated guesses can be made.

The most accepted date for the events is the patriarchal era. This would be time of Abraham, Isaac, and Jacob; however, as is discussed below, the highest probability would be around the time the Israelites were in Egypt a little later. The livelihood activities seem to be same as Abraham; that is, in raising large flocks and having many servants to tend them. There is no mention of any other of the prominent characters of the Bible. The covenant is not mentioned, nor is the law. There is nothing about the sojourn in Egypt; this would imply that the characters in the book were not part of that contingent. As far as we know there was no written law before the Exodus. It was a time when God spoke directly to a few individuals but the manner is not always given and is not the same in cases when He did. He spoke to Adam and Eve in the Garden of Eden but not necessarily face to face. It is uncertain exactly how He spoke to Cain in Genesis 4:9. The same is true for His conversations with Noah in Genesis 6–9 and with Abraham in Genesis 12 and 13. In Genesis 15:1 He spoke to Abraham in a vision. Other examples exist in Genesis of God's communications with Abraham. Later in the Old Testament, we find other methods like the burning bush to Moses, a still small voice to Elijah, and in visions to the prophets. In the Book of Job, God speaks to Job out of a whirlwind. All of these clues suggest the events in Job took place before Moses. Job could have even been a contemporary of Abraham's immediate descendants.

The time of the events would raise other questions to which no answers are given. To how many others did God speak directly with (including the time from Adam to Abraham)? How was the will of God made known to people, specifically ones like Eliphaz, Bildad, Zophar, and Elihu? Did the fact that there seemed to be a moral code, arise from Adam and Eve's eating of the forbidden fruit? Remember it was the tree of the knowledge of good and evil (Genesis 2:17). In the Book of Job there is a universal moral code that everyone is expected to follow. This code has not changed much through the ages. Every civilization has a similar code even if it is not always adhered to. If all of the characters in Job are related to Abraham, the knowledge of God and His will would have naturally been passed on orally.

The origin of the man, Job, or the region where is lived is not well defined. He is said to have lived in the land of Uz. For almost of the other important characters of the Bible, they are introduced by giving the name of their father. This is true for all of the books of the prophets except Daniel, Obadiah, and Haggai. Throughout the biblical narrative this is also usually the case. But in the Book of Job we have no clue to his ancestry. As a country Uz is mentioned two other times in the Bible, Jeremiah 25:20 and Lamentations 4:21. In Lamentations it is associated with Edom. It appears four times as the name of a person in a genealogy: Genesis 10:23, 1 Chronicles 1:17, Genesis 26:28, and 1 Chronicles 1:42. Because it is similar to Abram's home country of Ur, it is sometimes thought to be in the same region (but probably is closer to Edom). This area is roughly north of Babylon in what is now Iran. Job and Abram had the same occupation, so it is likely they could have lived in the same area.

Other clues come from the name of the homes and ancestors of the three friends who come to visit Job. The first mentioned is Eliphaz, the Temanite. There was a son of Esau named Eliphaz in Genesis 36. Esau and his family had moved away from Canaan and Jacob because "their possessions were too great for them to live together." This Eliphaz had a son named Teman from which the Eliphaz of Job might have come. We are not told where these descendants of Esau eventually lived. The second friend was Bildad the Shuhite. The term Shuhite came from Shuah who was one of the sons of Abraham and Keturah (Genesis 25:2). They also lived in the region of Edom. The third friend was Zophar, the Naamathite. Naaman (not the Syrian king healed by Elisha) was a son of Benjamin, Genesis 46:21, who also is thought to be from Edom. Thus the three friends (and perhaps Job himself) were probably descendants of Abraham and lived in the region of Edom. Edom is far away from the region of Ur; Edom is named after Esau, the twin brother of Jacob; Edom was his home after leaving Jacob. This is the region to the east and slightly south of the Dead Sea in what is now Jordan. The friends apparently knew each other and did not travel far to see Job. Thus is seems that Uz, the dwelling place of Job, was also near Edom. Job being called the richest man in the east would also point to Edom because it is east of the home of Jacob. If they were descendants of Abraham, this means the events in the Book of Job happened while the Israelites were in Egypt. It would also explain how they knew God and worshiped Him and place the timing around 1500 BC.

In chapters 32–37 we are introduced to a new character. This is the young man named Elihu. There appears to be five different men with the name. The first is listed in 1 Samuel 1:1 as being in the lineage of the prophet Samuel which would place him a couple of hundred years before David. He is referred to in 1 Chronicles 6 as Eliel and Eliab. Three others appear around the time of David; 1 Chronicles 12:20, 1 Chronicles 26:7, and 1 Chronicles 27: 18. None of these is the Elihu of Job. Job's Elihu is the son of Barachel of the family of Ram who is thought to be descended from Abram's brother Haran. The above is speculation, of course. With all the possible connections of all of the characters to Edom, it seems that original story of Job may have been an Edomite story, which would explain why there is no mention or connection to Israelite people or events. The placing of the time of the book during Israel's sojourn in Egypt would fit. Because of the inhabitants of Edom being related to Abraham, they also would have worshiped Jehovah.

That there were others who worshiped Jehovah is shown by a couple of other examples. In Genesis 14 Abram waged war with tribes that had captured Sodom and Gomorrah and taken Lot, Abram's nephew, captive. He was successful in his campaign to free Lot and took a lot of booty. As he returned he was met by Melchizedek who was described as king of Salem (Jeru-salem?) and priest of God most high. Abram gave him a tenth of all he had captured. No other details are given about Melchizedek in Genesis but he is referred to in Psalms 110:4 and Hebrews chapters 5, 6, and 7. In Hebrews Christ is compared to Melchizedek as a priest. Hebrews 7:6 explicitly states that Melchizedek was not of the genealogy of the Hebrews. In Exodus chapter 2 Moses flees to Midian and meets up with the family of Reuel and lives with them eventually taking a wife from one of the daughters. In Exodus 3:1 his father-in-law is called Jethro who is called the priest of Midian. These examples show the existence of other worshipers of Jehovah even to the extent of there being priests before the establishment of the Hebrew priesthood in Exodus. These two are mentioned in the Bible because of the intersection of their lives with the Hebrews. The Bible is the story only of the Hebrews. That is what makes the Book of Job more unique as there is no similar interaction with the Hebrews.

There is no mention of the age of Job when the events took place. Most often artists depicted Job as a very old man reminiscent of the way Father Time or the old year is depicted on New Year's Eve such as the series of works by William Blake mentioned earlier. He does seem to be the patriarch of his family. In those days the extended family usually lived together in a compound or other settlement or camp. Job's ten children lived within a short distance of him each in their own houses (1:4). However it is more likely that he was much younger. There is no mention of grandchildren or other descendants as there is in chapter 42. Eliphaz reminds him that the three friends are older than his father (15:10). And at the end Job lives for many, many more years.

Each time I do a study of the Book of Job, I discover different viewpoints. One question often asked is "How long did the events in the book take?" Again we have to rely on the few clues that are given. The travel time for the three friends could have been days or weeks. The time for the challenge to be made in heaven and the catastrophes carried out in chapters one and two is implied to be short. But the time that the suffering went on, the time the word spread to the friends, the time for journey preparations to made, and the time for the trip would be significant. As Job continues his lament in chapter three in rebuttal to the accusations made by Eliphaz in chapters 4 and 5, he describes months of suffering:

> So I am allotted months of emptiness, and nights of
> misery are apportioned to me. (Job 7:3)

In Job's summation in 29:2 he speaks of it being months since his pleasant days. His suffering has been going on long enough that he has become a target of ridicule (30:1–2). Also the debate could have been spread over time and the writing of it is a condensation of the proceedings. Thus its poetic form could no longer be an objection to the story being a relating of actual events.

That several details are omitted is a source of frustration to us because our curiosity wants to know those details. The Bible tends to not dwell on details that are not significant to the lesson being taught. For example, nothing is known of the life of Jesus between ages twelve and thirty. What did He do during that time? Or for that matter, what did He do from birth to age twelve? Again this provides room for a broad range of speculation. If we don't know, we can always make something up. That is suspected to be the case of a lot of ancient writings like in the Apocrypha and Pseudepigrapha.

Little is known when the story of Job came together. It undoubtedly existed in an oral version long before it was written down because the actual writing is generally believed to have been in the third century BC. Even the reference in James appears to be to an oral version because it says "you have heard of the steadfastness of Job," whereas most references in the New Testament to the Old Testament begin with "it is written." Whatever the method of conveyance and whatever time it was written, it was considered worthy of inclusion in the Old Testament. Some other inferior versions of the story of Job circulated in the early centuries BC that were rejected for inclusion in the Old Testament.

Absolutely nothing is known about who actually wrote down the version that we have today. Some scholars think there might have seen a slight corruption or tinkering with text by the scribes through the centuries or accidental errors propagated. The places pointed to are the apparently abbreviated speech of

Bildad in chapter 25, the missing third speech of Zophar, the last part of chapter 27 which is attributed to Job, but sounds more like one of the others, chapter 28 as an isolated discourse on wisdom, and the inclusion of the speech of Elihu in chapter 32 to 37 which is ignored elsewhere. There is nothing in these passages that is critical to the message of the book. When appropriate, the issues with these passages will be dealt with.

The Book of Job presents some unique problems of text and structure. The Hebrew is the most difficult in the Bible. Many words are found nowhere else and others are rarely used. This makes for variations in translations. Read as many Bible translations as possible because there is no guarantee that any one is more correct than another. I will mainly be using the NRSV even though new copies are hard to come by because I like the way it and the RSV read. Notice that there is no mention of the Jews, no promises of God to His people, no reference to great Israelites. The covenant name of God (Yahweh) is used only three times in the poetry (12:9; 20:23; 28:28). In some ways chapter 28 (speech on wisdom attributed to Job) does not seem to fit and is more like what we find in Proverbs. Elihu, who speaks more than the other three friends, is completely ignored in the rest of the book.

The traditional view of the man, Job, derives from chapters 1, 2, and 42; that is, as a paragon of patience. (There is some literature contemporary with the Old Testament that contains a version of Job; for example, one called *The Testament of Job.*) The rest of the book paints an entirely different picture. The Jewish scribes settled on the version we have in our Bibles. The biblical version provides us with a much deeper insight of our relationship with God and also with each other. That is why the book is timeless and furnishes a message to all generations. The lack of reference to time and place makes the book enduring and gives it an ability to speak to any age. The sound one makes celebrating the dropping an anvil on one's big toe expresses a timeless vocabulary.

The book is arranged into three distinct parts. The prologue of chapters 1 and 2 give the introduction and setting. The bulk of the book is contained in the dialogue in chapters 3 through chapter 28 and in the three discourses by Job (29–31), Elihu (32–37), and God (38–41). The dialogue is the heart of the book where the issues are raised and debated. In the epilogue in the last part of chapter 42 are the summations and conclusions. The prologue and epilogue are easy-to-read prose and form the basis of most peoples' understanding of the book. In so doing they miss the purpose of the book. The dialogue is very difficult Hebrew poetry. The rhyme is not in sounds but couplets of the same meaning. The construction in the poetry is three cycles of speeches followed by three discourses. Job speaks, is answered by one of the friends, he offers his rebuttal followed by another friend until the three cycles are complete. The last speech of the third friend Zophar is missing, leading some to think that chapter 27:13–23 might be Zophar speaking and not Job. The poetry ends with the three discourses. Of the forty-two chapters, twenty are attributed to Job, six to Elihu, four to God, four to Eliphaz, three to Bildad, two to Zophar, and three to the narrator of the prose. The description of events taking place in heaven shows that some, or all, of the book was given by inspiration.

We shall study the book as we have it. We will discover a Job you would never meet in the prologue and epilogue. As we will observe, Job is not a paragon of patience. Some have described Job as a rebel although the term dissident seems to fit better. A rebel usually wants to overthrow established authority while a dissident wants to change it from within. Notice the development in the speeches of Job and the increase in intensity (nothing much changes in the speeches of the friends except that they become more blunt). Job speaks truths evocative of every one's experience. The force of Job's arguments is not in personal tragedy, but its capacity to symbolize human outrage. It is an exposition of the way suffering people really feel when catastrophe strikes them. The language is of those shocked out of complacency that no reasonableness can justify. When one hits his thumb with a hammer, he tends to adopt a more vivid vocabulary.

The Book of Job provides a non-threatening basis for explor-
ing questions we might otherwise be hesitant to ask. Whom
do each of the characters typify? What is the significance of
God's questions to Job? What questions would he ask modern
mortals? Do mortals have a right to challenge God, to confront
divine authority? Should a person accept spiritual authority
when it is revealed in all its majesty? To what extent does
authority need challenge from below to establish its powers?
Does might make right? How much help can one expect from
authority when he opposes that authority? Whose side are you
on in the debate? The two weapons that Job has are his power
to withhold his allegiance and moral authority. To truly be able
to receive the message of the Book of Job, one needs to do what
should be done when reading any good story: allow yourself
to be absorbed in the characters and picture yourself as them.
As you read each character's utterances, imagine yourself as
being in the scene and experiencing what they are experiencing. As the story unfolds, see everything through their eyes and
perspective. In so doing you will be able to gain the enlighten-
ment the story of Job is meant to provide. You may even want
to assume the role of Satan to imagine what he was thinking
and why he was so negative.

Unless otherwise specified, all Scripture quotes are from the
Book of Job, New Revised Standard Version. Because I make
so many references to passages from the Book of Job, not all of
them are quoted. Therefore, having a copy of the Book of Job
handy as you read would be helpful.

CHAPTER 2

Setting the Stage

*The task of man is not to discover new worlds, but to discover
his own world in terms of human comprehension and beauty.*
—Archibald MacLeish

C hapters one and two introduce us to the main characters
of the book: Job, God, Satan, Eliphaz, Bildad, and Zophar
(Elihu is presented in isolation in chapters 32–37).

The first five verses of chapter one provide a description of
Job. He is said to be upright and blameless (as we go through
the book, notice that merely being mostly good would not
do). He is very religious and represents the ideal of practical
religion. He is very rich and powerful illustrating what blessed
"ought" to mean.

> There was once a man in the land of Uz whose name
> was Job. That man was blameless and upright, one
> who feared God and turned away from evil. There
> were born to him seven sons and three daughters. He
> had seven thousand sheep, three thousand camels,
> five hundred yoke of oxen, five hundred donkeys,
> and very many servants; so that this man was the
> greatest of all the people of the East. His sons used
> to go and hold feasts in one another's houses in turn;
> and they would send and invite their three sisters to
> eat and drink with them. And when the feast days
> had run their course, Job would send and sanctify

them, and he would rise early in the morning and offer burnt offerings according to the number of them all; for Job said, "It may be that my children have sinned, and cursed God in their hearts." This is what Job always did. (Job 1:1–5)

Verses 6–12 take place in heaven where a challenge is made. Satan is there; this not the Satan who is later identified as the Devil (although he may become that). The Hebrew word for Satan can be translated *the adversary* and some translations add the definite article *the* before Satan. It may perhaps be more of a title or position than an actual being, like Special Prosecutor or Inspector General. The Hebrew word for Satan is mentioned in only four verses in the Old Testament outside of Job and not translated as Satan in Psalms (Satan is much more prominent in the New Testament, where it seems to be interchangeable with the Devil).

They say, "Appoint a wicked man against him; let an accuser stand on his right." (Psalms 109:6)

Other times we see Satan working against someone:

Satan stood up against Israel, and incited David to count the people of Israel. (1 Chronicles 21:1)

Then he showed me the high priest Joshua standing before the angel of the LORD, and Satan standing at his right hand to accuse him. And the LORD said to Satan, "The LORD rebuke you, O Satan! The LORD who has chosen Jerusalem rebuke you! Is not this man a brand plucked from the fire?" (Zechariah 3:1–2)

The scene of God surrounded by His angels is similar to that when there was the discussion about how to deal with Ahab.

Then Micaiah said, "Therefore hear the word of the LORD: I saw the LORD sitting on his throne, with all the host of heaven standing beside him to the right and to the left of him. And the LORD said, 'Who will entice Ahab, so that he may go up and fall at Ramoth-gilead?' Then one said one thing, and another said another, until a spirit came forward and stood before the LORD, saying, 'I will entice him.' 'How?' the LORD asked him. He replied, I will go out and be a lying spirit in the mouth of all his prophets. Then the LORD said, 'You are to entice him, and you shall succeed; go out and do it.' So you see, the LORD has put a lying spirit in the mouth of all these, your prophets; the LORD has decreed disaster for you." (1 Kings 22:19–23)

A different Hebrew word is translated "devil" or "devils" four times in the Old Testament. Most of our concepts of the Devil and Satan (and even equating them) come from outside the Bible. The most influential are two epic poems and the folk tales about Faust. One poem is by the thirteenth century Italian poet known by (the easiest to remember and easiest to pronounce) part of his name "Dante." His was a three-part work called "The Divine Comedy" (comedy used here is a literary genre term, not humor). The part dealing most with Satan is called "Inferno." One will often hear references to "Dante's Inferno." The other work is by the eighteenth century English poet John Milton in two parts, "Paradise Lost" and "Paradise Regained." The image (mainly from Faust) is so ingrained that it is hard to picture him any other way than a red suit, tail, horns, and a pitch fork. The names "Lucifer" and Mephistopheles derive from these sources. Other images come from Revelation 12:7–9; 20:2–3. The New Testament provides a different picture (which is often in the plural): 1 Peter 5:8 "a roaring lion" and 2 Corinthians 11:14 "transformed into an angel of light," for example. In other words he probably won't appear as we expect him to or be readily obvious.

There is no reason given for the meeting in heaven in which the heavenly beings presented themselves to God. It is speculated that this was a standard procedure in heaven, that each of the beings had a particular assignment and occasionally reported on their activities. This would be why "Satan" is more of a title than a proper name. If the above conjectures are true, it appears that one of Satan's tasks is surveillance of the earth. God wants to be assured that Satan is doing a good job (1:7). If God is omniscient would He not know what Satan had been doing? Why did God have to ask? Perhaps Satan had specific duties and certain areas to keep tabs on. Speculation is interesting, but doesn't really provide any answers.

> The LORD said to Satan, "Where have you come from?" Satan answered the LORD, "From going to and fro on the earth, and from walking up and down on it." (Job 1:7)

If he has, he should be impressed by Job. However, Satan is very negative about Job's motivation. The distrust he developed about the motivation of humans might have come from his general surveillance during his rounds. Perhaps material wealth was the only measure of a person's worth that he observed being used. Worth is often assigned according to what can be measured and counted. Although Job's wealth is enumerated, God is careful to emphasize Job's righteousness and character. It would be uncertain whether the surveillance is only of individuals or every aspect of what is going on earth. It may also indicate that there are other realms in the universe besides the earth of which God is keeping track. The scene is repeated in chapter 2. There is no indication of the time lapse between the two meetings during which Job has been suffering from his losses, but he is apparently holding up well (it had to be long enough for a valid test). Satan is still as negative about Job's motivation as ever.

The assessment of Job's character given by God in chapter one needs to be remembered in reading the poetry. Satan, in his negativity, mocks God (keep this in mind) yet the challenge is accepted on Satan's terms with the stipulation that Job himself is not to be touched. (We should not be too critical of Satan; he was only playing the Devil's Advocate). In verses 1:13–19 a series of catastrophes befall Job. At least one of these is attributed to God (1:16). In a short time all of Job's possessions are wiped out. His family is wiped out. People of this time sought their immortality through their progeny, so the effect was very devastating. Job survives this first attack very well.

> Then Job arose, tore his robe, shaved his head, and fell on the ground and worshiped. He said, "Naked I came from my mother's womb, and naked shall I return there; the LORD gave, and the LORD has taken away; blessed be the name of the LORD." In all this Job did not sin or charge God with wrongdoing. (Job 1:20–22)

Verse 1:21 provides another popular visualization of Job. It has been taken out of context to use in hymns and spiritual songs ever since. To someone not familiar with the context, the sentiment could become confusing. What kind of God would give only to take away? That would seem to be a cruel and provocative action. Watch how Job's attitude gets modified through the poetry as he deals with this very question.

Sticking to his negative attitude, of chapter 2 Satan cries "foul" and the challenge is intensified. A couple of things to note in 2:3 are the mention of Job's integrity and that God says He moved against Job *without cause*. Satan proposes what he believes to be the ultimate challenge.

> The LORD said to Satan, "Have you considered my servant Job? There is no one like him on the earth, a blameless and upright man who fears God and turns away from evil. He still persists in his integrity, although you incited me against him, to destroy him for no reason." Then Satan answered the LORD, "Skin for skin! All that people have they will give to save their lives. But stretch out your hand now and touch his bone and his flesh, and he will curse you to your face." The LORD said to Satan, "Very well, he is in your power; only spare his life." (Job 2:3–6)

We see how the negative thoughts of Satan are used to induce God to accept the challenge. Job's misery increases.

Again considering the omniscience of God, didn't He already know what would happen in the test and that Job would survive the challenge? As in other instances in the Bible, it seems that God chooses not to know certain things. His knowing ahead of time how things would turn out would invalidate the test, and the same time, validate Satan's assertion. In verse 2:9, Job's integrity is specifically mentioned by his wife. She suggests that Job give up, curse God, and die. (This is interesting because it implies the thought if Job cursed God, God would take his life. Nothing like that is mentioned in the challenge. Soon we will see Job long for death.) Her motive may actually be beneficent, wanting to relieve him of his misery. We never hear from Satan again; perhaps his role in the drama that is the Book of Job is over. If Job thinks he has suffered up to now, he doesn't know the half of it. Just when Job thinks things couldn't get any worse, his three comforting friends prove him wrong. The friends prove to be Satan's most effective agents in their good intentions.

There is an implication to the challenge. Satan has claimed that people act only from selfish motives. The challenge sets out to prove the possibility, not the superiority of absolute justice. An attack is made on human worth and a defense is given. If Satan can discredit Job, he discredits humanity. He asks the question, "Can there be a truly righteous man?"

Up to this point Satan has been proven wrong in his assessment of human motivation for serving God. In chapter 3 we are suddenly shocked by the outcry from "patient" Job:

> After this Job opened his mouth and cursed the day
> of his birth. Job said: "Let the day perish in which
> I was born, and the night that said, 'A man-child is
> conceived.'" (Job 3:1–3)

For the first time, we see a negative thought expressed by Job. The thought will be repeated in the dialogue with the friends. In verses 3:4–10 he continues his rant against the day of his birth with very vivid descriptions of what he would like to happen to it. Job's cry becomes even stronger as he asks for death (3:1, 11, 16, 20–21). He sees death as a release from his suffering that is accessible to everyone, 3:16–19. In all of his raving, he never considers the possibility of taking his own life. The futility of such an action or losing his life in any way becomes apparent as he discusses his condition with his friends. A clue as to why Satan chose Job to be the subject of the challenge and why God let it happen is Job's statement in 3:25–26: "Truly the thing that I fear comes upon me, and what I dread befalls me. I am not at ease, nor am I quiet; I have no rest; but trouble comes."

As long as things are going well and we have a comfortable existence, we can be at peace. We can become so attached to the comforts that anxiety about losing them is a fear, even if subconsciously. As we go through the book, Job will change his mind about wanting to die. Look for Job's change of attitude and what brings it about.

There are two recognized great motivators for people. Satan used one of them in tormenting Job. Job had no idea why he was being subjected to pain and anguish, how long it might last, or who initiated it. This left him in a state of fear, the first great motivator as admitted in 3:25–26 above. Fear of losing possessions plagues many people and their anxiety robs them of the chance to enjoy what they have. Fear of losing health is a very strong one. Fear of losing loved ones ramps that up to a whole new level and is much harder to cope with. We have to do the best we can. Fear is a transitory motivation because as soon as the threat goes away, so does the response. A few years ago (2003, the SARS virus) when a virus threatened to become a world wild pandemic, there was an immediate rush to create a cure and a vaccine. When the threat subsided on its own, all support for research disappeared. Now when a new threat appears the rush for a vaccine and cure is reestablished. Had former work been continued, perhaps the world would have been prepared to deal with the new threat. People seem to only respond to an immediate danger.

The second great motivator was used by the Devil against Jesus in Matt. 4:1–11; Mark 1:12–13; Luke 4:1–13. He appealed to Jesus with the desire for great things. This motivation can produce both good and bad actions; it may inspire one to work hard and plan carefully, or it may cause one to cheat, steal, lie, and misuse others to achieve its end. Satan's assertion was that Job served God out of fear and desire.

We are driven by the same motivations. Our worry about the material should not be our guiding obsession. This was expressed by Jesus in the Sermon on the Mount which is summarized:

> Therefore do not worry, saying, "What will we eat?" or "What will we drink?" or "What will we wear?" For it is the Gentiles who strive for all these things; and indeed your heavenly Father knows that you need all these things. But strive first for the kingdom of God and his righteousness, and all these things will be given to you as well. (Matthew 6:31–33)

I once heard a motivational speaker talk about how attached we are to our material possessions. He suggested that if you have something whose loss would be devastating, you should go home and get rid of it. Otherwise the fear of losing it will be the source of constant anxiety. This is usually summed by asking, "Do you own your possessions, or do your possessions own you?" Like lots of other advice (not Jesus's, but that above) it is a lot easier to say than to do. If you do get rid of it you may spend your life regretting the decision. Such an action requires deep soul searching and commitment. On the other hand, if done thoughtfully and purposefully, it may bring a profound sense of relief and serenity to your life.

CHAPTER 3

The Initial External Assessment

Piety's hard enough to take among the poor who have to practice it. A rich man's piety stinks. It's insufferable.
—Archibald MacLeish

At the end of chapter two, Job is visited by three of his friends to comfort him.

> Now when Job's three friends heard of all these troubles that had come upon him, each of them set out from his home—Eliphaz the Temanite, Bildad the Shuhite, and Zophar the Naamathite. They met together to go and console and comfort him. When they saw him from a distance, they did not recognize him, and they raised their voices and wept aloud; they tore their robes and threw dust in the air upon their heads. They sat with him on the ground seven days and seven nights, and no one spoke a word to him, for they saw that his suffering was very great. (Job 2:11–13)

In chapter three Job goes to great lengths to express the depths of his anguish. He wants to leave no doubt as to his desperation. If he thinks he can get sympathy and pity from his friends, he is badly mistaken. He expected loyalty from them and assistance for his cause. This may remind of the phrase we often use of "fair weather friends"; or as Job will later insinuate, "with friends like these, who needs enemies?"

This was the time before the Exodus and Moses's writing of Genesis. However, the oral traditions and lore had been passed down. The great events of history up to that time were well known. God's dealings with people were common knowledge. Adam and Eve disobeyed God in Eden and were punished, Cain committed murder and was punished, Enoch was righteous and was rewarded, the people of Noah's day were evil and punished, Abram was righteous and given promises, Sodom and Gomorrah were wicked and punished, etc. From these and other examples, a doctrine of retribution was developed. One obeyed God and was rewarded; one disobeyed and was punished. The rewards and punishment were meted out immediately or very soon; the concept of an afterlife was not expressed. The rewards or punishment often involved one's progeny. It is not surprising, then, that Job and his friends believed in a rigid doctrine of retribution; you were good then you enjoyed life; you were bad then you suffered. This is the very doctrine that Satan was attacking. This is the climate in which the three friends offer their advice. It is often stated:

> Honor the LORD with your substance and with the first fruits of all your produce; then your barns will be filled with plenty, and your vats will be bursting with wine. My child, do not despise the LORD's discipline or be weary of his reproof, for the LORD reproves the one he loves, as a father the son in whom he delights. (Proverbs 3:9–12)

We will see, as the discussions in the dialogue proceed, a gradual shift in Job's position. The three friends remain largely unaffected. We saw in chapter 3 how Job began in despair (after the friends had come to comfort him). He wished for death. His attitude will move into outrage—why is he singled out? (As a footnote, he will never be told). Then his attitude hardens into resolution—God must prove that He is just. There is no real development in the friend's arguments. They begin with a show of comfort, proceed to inference, and emerge into outright accusations. We will also notice the same progression as we go from one friend to the next. Eliphaz is the most general, Bildad is a little more specific, and Zophar attacks Job more personally. Their beginning comments in the first round of speeches are of a generic nature; the wicked have bad things happen to them. In the second round of speeches the sins committed by the wicked are more specific as are the punishments. When Job ignores the fact that they are pointing out the reasons for his troubles, they accuse Job of specific sins and specific retributions are described; Eliphaz's accusations are rather harsh in chapter 22. To be fair to the friends, they believe there is a solution to Job's problems and they are happy to deliver it. Job at first searches for pity from his friends (6:14; 19:21), but does not get it. As the friends present their case Job debates with them but at times ignores them and directs his pleas heavenward. Finally in chapters 29–31 Job presents a challenge to God.

The friends hold to the tradition view; they have no reason to question it. They are very dogmatic and conservative; as such they represent all who hold similar views. They point out that it has always worked in the past. Even Job had once agreed with them. How can he risk overthrowing this long-established order of things? Why does he not recognize that it cannot be abandoned just to accommodate him? They echo the force of the community ethos and opinion. If the majority believes it, they must be speaking for God; they become His voice in the matter. Their case is already established in history and needs no further refinement.

It comes as a shock when one finds their experience is contrary to what they rightfully expected. Job represents all that have had that happen. A faith is supposed to provide comfort and solace. What happens when it seems to actually make things worse? How can one justify it? The guidance offered by our religion must prove true and helpful if we are to take it seriously. People, even today, reject religion if they think it is irrelevant to their lives. They want to see it work now.

Our generations are seeking instant gratifications and knowledge; they should only be a mouse or key click away. Job had never worried about such things, but is forced into it by the dialogue with the friends. Their negative attitude may, therefore, be important to Job after all; he probably never would have examined his faith otherwise.

Satan's challenge did not allow God to offer any help or comfort to Job; He must recluse Himself from the trial. Job had always believed that God was responsible for his wellbeing because of his lifestyle. The catastrophes indicate that God had withdrawn His aid. Job felt lost, abandoned, without direction. He believed that God was still present, but had a changed nature toward him. No one else had the power to do what had happened to him. Is the God Job once knew no more, and must he seek another? No. Job pursued the God he knew.

CHAPTER 4

The Attack on Job Begins

We have no choice but to be guilty. God is unthinkable if we are innocent.
—Archibald MacLeish

Presumably Eliphaz is the oldest and he speaks first in chapters four and five. The other two will not disagree with him. Verse 4:2 is classic; Eliphaz begins very politely and innocently enough:

> If one ventures a word with you, will you be offended?
> But who can keep from speaking? (Job 4:2)

The last half of the verse says it all. Does this feeling ever occur to you? Eliphaz begins by pointedly reminding Job of his former status (4:3–5). Remember this passage when we get over to chapter 22. Job is accused of being impatient (4:5). But then we see the negative attitude taking over. The precedent has been established for the other two friends to follow. Based upon the retribution system, the friends know exactly what has happened. The details may be missing, but they can and will thoughtfully supply them.

Eliphaz insists that, whatever the appearances, justice is always carried out (4:8). Job would like for such a system to be in effect, but instead they terrify him with visions (4:12ff; see also 7:14). Even so, people are categorically wrong before God and have no reason for complaint (4:17–19; 5:8–16). Eliphaz points out that there is no heavenly help for Job (5:1). (Because this was a time of polytheism and all sorts of gods in other cultures, this could be referring to one of them. However, Job does not attribute power to anyone but Jehovah.) This may have given Job an idea, though, that we will see develop. But Eliphaz knows that attitudes can be harmful. Job 5:2 says, "Surely vexation kills the fool, and jealousy slays the simple."

Does the advice he gives in 5:8 ("As for me, I would seek God, and to God I would commit my cause") sound like the advice we often try to give people (also see 22:21)? Actually that is exactly what Job is going to do but not in the sense Eliphaz intended. After all, the righteous are cared for (5:17–26). He does offer something that Job needs:

> You shall be hidden from the scourge of the tongue.
> (Job 5:21)

How does Eliphaz know what he says is true and why does he say it?

> See, we have searched this out; it is true. Hear, and
> know it for yourself. (Job 5:27)

The fundamental outrage of Job's agonies he conceives to be insult. The object of his efforts is justification and reconciliation. He considers that he is a victim of God (6:4; 7:20). This explains why his words at times may have seemed rash (6:3). At this point he still asks for death as a way to end his suffering (6:8–9). He admits in verse 6:11 that he is not patient. In 6:14–23 he elaborates on his great loss of status. In doing so he begins with a warning to the friends (6:14) and ends with how he sees their attitude (6:21). He has certainly done no wrong (6:24). Because of his desperation, he is not responsible for what he says (6:26; 7:20). And in spite of the fact that the friends are no real comfort, he does not want them to leave (6:28–30).

Chapter 7 is concerned with Job's reflection on the futility of human existence (especially 7:1–2; 7:9). He would certainly like to regain his status but thinks that the possibility is zero

(7:7) and death is imminent. But death underscores the futility he feels. Job begins to realize that death would remove all hope of vindication.

> Remember that my life is a breath; my eye will never again see good. The eye that beholds me will see me no more; while your eyes are upon me, I shall be gone. As the cloud fades and vanishes, so those who go down to Sheol do not come up; they return no more to their houses, nor do their places know them any more. (Job 7:7–10)

(He will elaborate as the debate continues). It is a predicament implicit in all human life. Mortals are stricken from birth with the blight of mortality. Job's complaints are against God (7:11–20). This is one of those places where his remarks seem to be directed to God or at least to God through the friends. Job wonders why God should even care:

> What are human beings, that you make so much of them, that you set your mind on them, visit them every morning, test them every moment? (Job 7:17–18)

Compare this passage with Psalm 8. He is not asking for eternal life, but only a return to the life he had before (7:16). God is too important and has better things to do than to worry about the trivial sins of a man (7:20). If something is wrong the easy thing for God to do is to pardon him. Otherwise Job will lapse in oblivion (7:21).

Perhaps the best explanation of why we have the Book of Job in our Bibles is given in reference 1, page 50:

> The extraordinary predicament of Job is not intended to lift him out of the experience of ordinary man. His catastrophes merely represent objectively that which occurs subjectively in one's own universe when tragedy strikes. The outcry of Job is expressive of the common experience of the race.

Hardly anyone considers that he is getting what he deserves when calamity occurs. It does not matter whether he does or does not in fact. The rationalization that one forms in his mind is the way he views reality. You do not have to be as blameless as Job to feel that an injustice is done to you. Even hardened, proven criminals often take this stance.

The idea of calling someone a windbag is not new. Bildad uses this description of Job. We will see it used again by Eliphaz in 15:2 and Job returns the favor in 16:3. These and other exchanges give the idea that the debate was lively and, at times, heated and the friends are still negative. Apparently though, there was not the current tendency to constantly interrupt. Each was allowed to have his say.

According to the three friends, God always deals out absolute justice. The only reason one would suffer greatly is if a person is evil (8:3). Bildad does allow the possibility that Job lost his children because of their own sins (8:4). The solution is very simple and easy; Job must repent and return to God (8:5–7). To us this may sound like very good advice; in fact, we offer similar thoughts today to people who are having difficulties. The impact may be the same on them that it was on Job if they feel they were basically following God.

For proof of his views, Bildad appeals to history (8:8–10). Our lifetime is too short to gather all that wisdom from our own experience, so we consider what has happened throughout history. Bildad insists that history makes sense. He uses the analogy of papyrus to strengthen his point. Just as dryness in the papyrus indicates that the water is gone, so people who are blighted witness the absence of God (8:11–19). This shows that those who forsake God will perish.

God is completely fair. If one is blameless, God will not reject him (8:20). (Job has been called blameless by God in 1:8.) However God will avoid the evildoers. Job has obviously been rejected by God and must, therefore, just as obviously, be evil. Job is wrong and must repent of his wrongdoing; then his life will be restored.

> See, God will not reject a blameless person, nor take
> the hand of evildoers. He will yet fill your mouth
> with laughter. (Job 8:21)

All the torments of Job strike ultimately at his honor. Job will try to defend his honor and maintain his integrity because one may have integrity, meaning unity of character, and still not be honorable; standing for and doing the right thing because it is right in itself. Even honor can mean different things to different people; our everyday usage of the word can dilute its value. A person in a position of power can be referred as "The Honorable . . ." or "His or Her Honor" when the person's character is anything but. Throughout history people have valued their or their family's honor to the point of sacrificing themselves for it. Defending honor does not necessarily mean the cause is just. Feuds have gone on for generations long after the original cause has been forgotten. Tensions remain between countries because each feels it has an honor to defend (when maybe it is really just pride).

Individuals want honor as a way of being reassured they really are worth something, that they are somebody. Satan had insisted that humans are interested only in their own wellbeing, "skin for skin" (2:4). This is the premise used to justify torture to obtain information from prisoners and others. In fact, isn't this what is happening to Job? Pleasure, security, or status is not the source of honor; but rather, honor may be maintained at the loss of reputation. Otherwise, one's worth, from which one's moral basis in derived, would only depend on the opinion of others. All codes of conduct ultimately rest on the honor of people because they cannot be enforced without it. Things that are repressive to the individual are often rationalized away. An example is seen in the compliance to speed limits on roads; even though they are imposed for the general safety, they are routinely ignored. Rules and restrictions imposed during a pandemic are seen as repressive, so there are those who ignore and protest against them even though it is for their own (and others) health. Honor cannot be created to serve an end, but is transmitted in tradition. It rests on real foundations. We cannot conjure it up to meet a need or serve a purpose, it must be a part of our basic makeup.

Job is willing to admit that, as a human being, he cannot be perfectly just before God:

> Indeed I know that this is so; but how can a mortal
> be just before God? (Job 9:2)

God is too powerful to be reached on human terms. No one exercises control over God (9:3–12, 19). Job readily admits the overwhelming power of God. It puts Him beyond human coercion, but also beyond understanding of human frailty. Being great enough to help Job, God is too remote to understand a mortal's needs. So Job asks not how can a person be justified before God, but how can one argue their case with God so as to justify themselves. Thus God lacks the capacity to deal justly. There is the added insult that Job must appeal for mercy from his accuser (9:15). Even if Job were able to present his own case, his words would be used against him (9:20). God even laughs at the innocent:

> When disaster brings sudden death, he mocks at the
> calamity of the innocent. (Job 9:23)

Job doubts that he will ever get a fair hearing (9:25–31). This leads to periods of hopelessness. Rather than wallow in such depressing thoughts, he desperately seeks a solution. The old system of retribution does not provide one, so he must seek it in radically different systems. Before suffering and injustice had been imposed upon him, he had no need for other systems. His integrity is the only foundation upon which a solution can be based. Since there is a gap between God and humans, Job becomes aware of what is lacking in the old system. He has overlooked the possibility that there could be an arbitrator between them:

> For he is not a mortal, as I am, that I might answer
> him, that we should come to trial together. There is

no umpire between us, who might lay his hand on
us both. (Job 9:32–33)

Job does not really believe there is such an arbitrator
because there was no need for one before; if there were one
he would not be so confused about what is happening to him
and feel such deep despair. Even though negativism controls
most of his thoughts there is a positive assertion implied in it:
there ought to be an arbitrator! This idea is introduced because
it really shows how extreme his condition has become. Once
that is realized perhaps his undeserved punishment will be
withdrawn. But Job is afraid to speak to God:

> If he would take his rod away from me, and not let
> dread of him terrify me, then I would speak without
> fear of him, for I know I am not what I am thought
> to be. (Job 9:33–35)

How can such a small being have dealings with God?
Religious discussions can be carried on reasonably as long as
the issues are not vital. If only things really worked the way
the friends are insisting that they work (and, incidentally, the
way Job would like for them to work) negotiations could be
carried on without fear.

Chapter 10 deals with man's relationship with God. Job
asks, "Why me?" (10:1–3). There is a big problem because God
cannot talk like a human (10:4–7). (This illustrates why it was
important for Jesus to come in the flesh; we now have a way of
knowing that God has seen things from our perspective!) God
seems to be destroying His fairest work (10:8–13). He knows
its terrible end. How can God fashion the human body with
such care (Genesis 2:7), knowing well the horrible dissolution
to come? A mortal is in disgrace whether good or bad (10:15).
Thus Job wants some life for restoration to occur (10:20).

In spite of being abandoned by his friends, Job could handle
that well enough. His outcry is for an answer to his problem
and he knows that to receive an answer, he must stubbornly
cling to life. Anguish and loss are bad enough, but the real

issue is insistence on his integrity by which his honor may be made known. What about the honor of a God who allows such torment? How does one know of the existence of God if not through one's own experience? In Job's former state, things made sense and were predictable, but now he does not discern what the pattern or divine strategy is. Job admits the overwhelming majesty of God. Destroying his fairest work does not glorify Him.

Zophar begins to make specific accusations against Job. To begin with, what he has been saying is utter nonsense (11:2–3). Job has been saying that he is blameless in God's sight (11:4). (Which is true!) Job has been wanting God to speak to him to tell him what he has done wrong. Zophar also wants God to speak to Job, but expects a different conversation. Actually, at the end they will both be surprised. Only God has complete understanding and wisdom:

> But O that God would speak, and open his lips
> to you, and that he would tell you the secrets of
> wisdom! For wisdom is many-sided. (Job 11:5–6a)

Notice the very comforting words that Zophar has for Job.

> Know then that God exacts of you less than your
> guilt deserves. (Job 11:6b)

We can become just as judgmental as Zophar. God's majesty puts Him beyond appeal and any comprehension by humans (11:7–12). In comparison to God, mortals are nothing. God is quick to recognize sin and deals out the punishment (11:11). Presumably, Job fits the category. It will be a long time before any person gets understanding.

For the three friends, as expressed here by Zophar (11:13–20), the solution to Job's problems is simple. He must admit that he is a sinner and turn to God. We should realize that when we offer platitudes and pat answers to someone; they may receive the advice just as Job did from his friends. Zophar considers that no complaint from a suffering person is valid.

Job therefore must be a sinner and deserves death. He is lucky to be alive because God is being merciful (11:6b).

The Book of Job asserts the worth of a person in themselves, not their capacity to produce goods. Job's integrity is the source of his worth. He maintains the same standards regardless of the situation; he will be consistent in his dealings. Others may be consistently bad, but that is not how Job operates. He stands for what is moral and true.

How one looks at integrity depends on society. If an evil person prospers, it indicates there is no underlying moral order in human (not Christian) affairs. If an evil person prospers in evil society, the world is out of step or goodness is not grounded in reality. In our time people seem to differentiate between a public and private integrity. What an official does in private is of no concern to the public as long as it does not directly affect them. Thus one may have an integrity which reflects unity of society. How much value do you think is placed on integrity today? Without a test of integrity, an inner weakness may not be apparent. Then one is in personal jeopardy because the first real challenge may threaten not only their possessions and attainments, but their very identity.

Integrity is, after all, a private, internal matter, but it is expressed in human relationships. Honor expresses consistent and helpful actions toward others. An honorable person does not sacrifice integrity for it would destroy their identity. Gaining honor usually means that reputation has improved. (It does not mean they have necessarily improved because others may not value integrity). People who have no inner conviction of spiritual worth lose their identity. Therefore, they seek it from society. The approval of others becomes a necessity to them. Job is obviously upset by Zophar's pointed accusations that Job is a sinner. Thus Job becomes a little harsher in his replies to the friends. He begins by addressing their attitude that they are the only ones who have wisdom. I love the sarcasm:

> No doubt you are the people, and wisdom will die
> with you. (Job 12:2)

Job is quick to point out that the things they have been saying are common knowledge (12:3) and they are no better than he (13:2). Job has lost his status, and those around him are ready to use it as a basis for contempt (12:4–6). Isn't this next statement so true of people?

> Those at ease have contempt for misfortune, but it
> is ready for those whose feet are unstable. (Job 12:5)

It is beginning to dawn on Job that there really are injustices to be found in the world. A negative thought that might not have occurred to him before his troubles began. There is no doubt in Job's mind who is responsible for what has happened; only God has the ability and power (12:7–12). To prove that he can quote authority as well as the friends, Job tells how God actually has picked on everyone (12:12–25). It is in his power to do so. Job has been a keen observer of God at work (13:1). Growing tired of the friend's arguments, Job wants to take his case directly to God (13:3, 15). The friends have been absolutely no help. Great sarcasm again:

> As for you, you whitewash with lies; all of you are
> worthless physicians. If you would only keep silent,
> that would be your wisdom! (Job 13:4–5)

Even though the friends claim they speak for God, Job does not allow them that complacency (13:7–9). God's reputation is in more danger from His defenders than from His attackers. Therefore, God will rebuke them (13:10). Compare with 42:7. The incapacity of Job's friends to comfort him illustrates that it is people who carry out most cruelly and effectively what they conceive to be the just judgments of God. Insult stings most when it comes from one's peers. Consider how this applies, for example, in disagreements in the church. The wisdom the friends offer is rubbish:

> Your maxims are proverbs of ashes, your defenses
> are defenses of clay. (Job 13:12)

Job apparently stops an interruption (13:13) and starts explaining how he will present his case (13:14–19). By the time he has finished he has turned from addressing the friends and is directing his comments to God. What are his sins, anyway (13:23)? Those of his youth (13:26)? Naturally a good man is not perfect in the absolute sense. God is really rather demeaning Himself (13:25).

After exhibiting such confidence, Job lapses back into negative thoughts (13:27–28). One's life is short, underscoring the futility of it all (14:1–3). Because life is so short, one ought to be able to enjoy what there is of it (14:4–6). Mortals have no hope; Job emphasizes his futility by contrasting the example of the fate of a tree with that of a person; a tree that is cut down will often sprout and grow again (14:7–12) (for me maybe a dandelion would be a better example). Again turning his pleas to heaven Job now begs for life (14:13–17). The great question Job asks should make us appreciate what we have in Christ:

> If mortals die, will they live again? All the days of my
> service I would wait until my release should come.
> (Job 14:14)

Job desires resurrection, not as compensation for what he has suffered, but so that he can be justified. So radical is this thought that nothing in human experience could conceivably merit it. He is not seeking merely a release from pain. He wants life, real life beyond death, not a paradise or return of possessions. He is willing to spend some time in Sheol if that would help (14:13–15).

But all is hopeless (14:18–21) because God destroys hope (14:19). Thus the answer to the question 14:14 is a "no." (It might be instructive to look at John 11:25 and 2 Tim. 1:10). By his own admission, Job has become a whimpering, self-centered creature.

> They feel only the pain of their own bodies, and
> mourn only for themselves. (Job 14:22)

And thus at the completion of the first round of the dialogue between Job and his friends, he feels no better. Their arguments have not had the desired effect. Will they modify their positions in order to better reach him?

This is the assessment of Job's life through chapter 14. He started out described as being very wealthy but also being very pious. God even acknowledged him as being upright and without blame. Satan gives the negative opinion that Job only serves God for what he can get out of him. Everyone has their price. Love based only upon what another can give you is not very stable; take away what they can give, and the love withers. This analogous to when one of the party demands something like "if you really loved me, you would . . ." This should be a red flag to the other member whose response maybe should be "If you really loved me, you would not ask me to do that."

Look what happened to Adam when he did what Eve asked him to do. Adam ate the forbidden fruit and was punished along with Eve. They succumbed to the desire to be like God in knowing good and evil. The human tendency is to do what they conceive as being best for themselves. Satan wants to test Job on this premise. At first all Job's material possessions are taken away in a series of disasters, one right after the other. These could probably be dispensed with easily enough but the forth disaster is the depriving him of his children. Still Job manages to cope bravely enough. Since Job did not succumb to those torments, Satan insists on a more personal attack. This is like when a prisoner is tortured to get them to reveal secrets or confess to a crime. This tactic does not break Job either. He does however wish for release from his pain and suffering. The easiest escape would be if he had never been born or been still born. The severity of the attacks and the suddenness of them indicate that it is not mere coincidence. Job knows of only one source powerful enough to bring it all about. Through the dialogue he will confront God with this possibility.

Three friends come to console and comfort him. They begin, and will continue with, a very negative attitude. Job used to uphold and sustain others, but now that is has come to him, he is impatient. Then the friends espouse the doctrine of retribution that all of them have believed. Only those who are wicked suffer and the severity is proportional to the seriousness of the sin. Job catches the subtlety of the message right away; he is suffering greatly therefore he must have sinned greatly. The force of this negative assertion is very powerful; he now thinks he is being punished for no reason. His reaction is one of anger and despair. If God is responsible for his circumstances, Job feels he is too weak compared to God to do anything about it and demands a fair trial because he is sure God would show him favor and vindicate him.

Another hope that sprang from his despair was for an afterlife. Nothing in the conventional retributive pattern held by Job and his friends either demanded or could give basis for a restoration of life after death. Death will not be a harvest as described in 5:26; not a granary but a prison. Life after death becomes a doctrine of spiritual significance, not as an end, but as an indispensable precondition to personal reconciliation with God. It can neither be deserved by human merit not can it compensate for history's injustices.

The very violence of Job's denunciation of the ways of God belies his claim that a mortal is a minute and valueless object. He asserts the lost dignity of humans.

CHAPTER 5

Round Two

If God is God He is not good, if God is good He is not God; take
the even, take the bad."
—Archibald MacLeish, from the dialogue of the play J. B.

E liphaz disputes the defense Job makes. In fact, Eliphaz considers it so bad that he questions why he should even answer it (15:1–3). If what Job says is true, why would anyone fear God (15:4)? In defending himself, Job is actually condemning himself (15:5–6). Job has no reason to be so arrogant (15:7–9). The friends have much better qualifications to judge the matter than Job (15:10). After all, the friends are only saying what God would say if he were to speak (15:11). How often is that our attitude when we are arguing with someone? The friends presume the role of God. Certain that they are right, they make judgments and offer terms.

From the description of Job that Eliphaz gives in 15:12–13, Job has not taken too kindly to his admonitions. If they are to have a meaningful discussion, Job needs to calm down and view the situation more objectively and think things through more deeply. However, when one is suffering excruciating pain it is hard to concentrate on nobler thoughts. Job becomes another person, a prisoner of tortured nerve and tissues, no longer in command of the sensitive machinery of his conscious being; he is pettish, self-contradictory, and irrational. A mortal is necessarily unclean before God (15:14–16), thus the righteousness of which the friends speak is not merely acquittal from a given charge. Eliphaz justifies what he is about to say:

> I will show you; listen to me; what I have seen I will declare—what sages have told, and their ancestors have not hidden, to whom alone the land was given, and no stranger passed among them. (Job 15:17–19)

Then he proceeds to elaborately describe the gloomy prospects of the wicked (15:20–35). The conditions Eliphaz describes are a lot like the condition Job is in right now. If one is not careful, their entire lives can be built upon externals such as reputation and wealth rather than their inner being. This can create great anxiety that we saw Job express (3:25). Trying to please a multitude of external masters usually results in pleasing no one.

One's very being becomes rooted in something or someone outside themselves. There is a constant struggle to force one's behavior to conform to what is expected. Being dependent upon perceived patterns of living to gain approval and respect can cause one to both despise and resent those who expect it. Once one relies on external influences to define their being, they become an ever-present threat because they may be withdrawn at any time. One may be deluded by their own success into confounding the symbols of worth with worth itself. The only self they know becomes attached to much goods (Luke 12:13–21). "Take away the barns," and self vanishes into nothingness.

Our task is to believe ourselves to be of worth in spite of outward evidences that we are. One must not belong to possessions. We only possess them if their loss does not threaten us. If we cannot dispense with then, we cannot control them; hence, cannot own them. We discussed a proposed solution to this problem in chapter 2. If it is a relationship we fear losing, then we should nurture it to the best of our abilities. If it is lost in spite of our best effort, then we are better off without it because it would be a constant threat to us.

Similarly, we must not be a slave to reputation. For then we would merely mirror community opinion and not possess convictions of our own. (All things can be ours if we are Christ's [1 Corinthians 3:4–23].) The power beyond is the sole dependable basis upon which we can save ourselves from being strangled by our own success.

The friends treat Job, not as one in need, but as a faulty theological proposition. They have not done a good job of comforting him:

> I have heard many such things; miserable comforters are you all. (Job 16:2)

Job considers the friends words as so much hot air (16:3), and he wonders why they even bother to speak. It is a lot easier to condemn when you are on the outside looking in:

> I also could talk as you do, if you were in my place; I could join words together against you, and shake my head at you. I could encourage you with my mouth, and the solace of my lips would assuage your pain. (Job 16:4–5)

But Job has real needs. Nothing has eased his pain (16:6, 12). It is savage and relentless. Job has no doubt that he has become a victim of God (16:7–17). He has been so severely assailed that he is worn out. People have turned against him and may even physically assault him (16:10). God is using him for target practice (16:13 also see 6:4).

Job cries out for help:

> O earth, do not cover my blood; let my outcry find no resting place. Even now, in fact, my witness is in heaven, and he that vouches for me is on high. My friends scorn me; my eye pours out tears to God, that he would maintain the right of a mortal with God, as one does for a neighbor. (Job 16:18–21)

The idea of not letting his blood be covered by the earth comes from Genesis 4:10. As long as it is not covered it will continue to cry out. Then he looks to heaven for the restoration of human dignity. (See Hebrews 9:24). The friends had previously warned him against trying this (5:1). Where does Job get this new found confidence? There is no evidence that the heavenly witness exists. He reaches his position on basis of what ought to be. There has to be a rescue for the righteous.

Job abandons his confidence almost as soon as he has expressed it. In verses 17:1–2, he reverts to his fatalistic, negative conclusions. The friends have provided no help (17:3–5). Perhaps it is because God has closed their eyes or because they hope to get a share of his property. God is responsible for his condition, as Job sees it, but the righteous have made their own contributions to it (17:6–12). Job rebukes his attackers:

> But you, come back now, all of you, and I shall not
> find a sensible person among you. (Job 17:10)

Job now realizes that the grave not only represents the death of the flesh, but also the death of hope and dignity (17:13–16). In 17:13 the place where Job expects to go when he dies is often translated as "grave." The NRSV merely transliterates the Hebrew word as "Sheol." This is neither a place of punishment nor reward; it is simply the place to which one goes when they die. One does not have consciousness there. In 17:14 a different Hebrew word is used; translated "pit" in the NRSV and as "corruption" in NIV and others, but it is basically the same idea.

Job's agony is not small; the capacity to suffer greatly (to know the bitterness of high outrage) draws him from an early posture of self-deprecation to assert once again the lost dignity of humans. No longer is he resigned to death and extinction. If he dies and vanishes away, he will never be vindicated. From this point on we see him growing stronger and stronger as the debate progresses until he presents a bold challenge to God in chapters 29–31.

It is inconceivable to the friends that Job still doesn't get it. They can't understand why he is so agitated:

> How long will you hunt for words? Consider, and
> then we shall speak. Why are we counted as cattle?
> Why are we stupid in your sight? You who tear

yourself in your anger—shall the earth be forsaken because of you, or the rock be removed out of its place? (Job 18:2–4)

The fact that Job does not follow the friends' advice shows what a bad attitude he has. He obviously considers them stupid, but, in reality, he is only being stubborn. It is pretty arrogant to expect the whole moral order of things to be undone for Job.

Bildad repeats the gloomy, negative prospects for the wicked (18:5–21). This theme is taken up by all three of the friends. Compare chapter 18 with chapters 16 and 20. This description also closely parallels Job's condition. By describing Job's sufferings, the three friends have only added to them. There is a lesson for us when we try to comfort others. Be careful that our consoling does not add to the burden. After all, Job's problems are all his own doing (18:7–8). Evil man is executed by his own fiendish devices. Job will not be remembered any more (18:17) and he has no surviving offspring (18:19). That is precisely what is starting to bother Job.

The three lieutenants of God minister to the theological needs of Job. They are sure that absolute justice is being carried out—regardless of appearances. Their view is easy to hold when dealing only with appearances. There is never any mention of the friends trying to minister to Job's physical needs.

Job experiences evil as a reality. He cannot accept the platitudes of the past. He will not defend the honor of God at the expense of denying his own innocence. He will not allow himself violently to be forced into a dogmatic system. It is easy today to become so engrossed in defending the system we embrace that we can overlook the actual human needs of others. Though Job was in physical torment, people can also suffer emotional and mental torments that are just as devastating. Even though we don't intend it, our insensitive comments, attitudes, and comforts can only greatly increase the suffering of those we presume to help. Just like people today, Job was looking for sympathy, and perhaps even a little empathy, not advice on how much stronger his faith needed to be.

One can perhaps accept the wrath of authority when they know they have done something wrong. They may even be able to accept the rejection of others. In times past (and maybe still today in certain places) punishment is ordered to be carried out by their peers. The range of punishment was from public humiliation such as being placed in stocks to death such as by stoning. What people can't accept is being disciplined when they are innocent. Punishment is expected to be meted out by authorities and to be unpleasant if it is intended to be a deterrent to others. The greatest torment comes from one's peers:

> How long will you torment me, and break me in pieces with words? These ten times you have cast reproach upon me. (Job 19:2–3)

> All my intimate friends abhor me, and those whom I loved have turned against me. (Job 19:19)

I tried to count to see if there really were ten times or if that was an exaggeration for emphasis. The number is not too far off. The translation can be "cast reproach" or "insulted." Even if Job has committed some sin, it has not been an external thing (19:4) and did not affect anyone else (compare 7:20 and 13:26). The friends look down upon him only because of his condition (19:5). A little later in this chapter (19:21–22) Job says the friends allow him no peace. Repeating from earlier: "The incapacity of Job's friends to comfort him illustrates that it is man himself who carries out most cruelly and effectively what he conceives to be the just judgments of God."

It is God, Job says, that put him in the wrong while it is really God who is in the wrong (19:6–22). Job has aired his complaint but there has been no answer:

> Even when I cry out, "Violence!" I am not answered; I call aloud, but there is no justice. (Job 19:7)

Job is a victim of heaven. There is no escape. No one dare pity him. Job has been abandoned by the whole human community (19:13–20). He asks for their pity (19:21–22). There is no court of appeals. Job has been honorable; why hasn't God? Job had lived in a sensible, predictable world under the care of a dependable God. A person got what they deserved (and what Job deserves is restoration to his former position). Though Job is at odds with fate and his times, he cannot console himself because he is linked by his integrity to a moral order which will finally be triumphant. No evidence remains of such an order. He has been flung athwart of the whole stream of things. Job demands that God vindicate Himself by vindicating Job. To restore honor to Job is to establish the honor of God.

Job does not want his arguments to simply pass away; he wants them preserved (19:23–24). In order for that to happen, Job needs a champion. He thus asserts the existence of a redeemer:

> For I know that my Redeemer lives, and that at the
> last he will stand upon the earth. (Job 19:25)

Contrast the redeemer with the witness of chapter 16. The redeemer is the friend as contrasted with Eliphaz, Bildad, and Zophar. Some translations use the word "avenger" which seems more appropriate as seen in verse 19:29. (Compare with Hebrews 7:25). The real work of a Israelite redeemer is probably best described in the Book of Ruth. Hardly a merciful figure, he brings about justice to his own kindred. He is the executor of "an eye for an eye" and is certainly not the Jewish Messiah. Christians have appropriated the word for Christ as was popularized in Handel's "Messiah." This is not the way the word is used in Job. It is perfectly okay to adopt the concept to one's own condition. After all, that is what makes the Book of Job such an enduring work and why it has had such wide spread appeal. At any stage in our lives we can read into it our own condition and find solace in it. Otherwise the book is of no value.

Fundamentally, though, verses 19:23–29 present a threat. Job's words have been disregarded or mishandled by men; God has not heard him. He wants his case preserved. The Redeemer will stand beside Job or cause God to stand beside him. The friends should be afraid. The judgment mentioned here is probably temporal, not eternal.

Now we can understand why Job has such mood swings and why he drops his hope so suddenly. Verses 19:23–29 are cited to strengthen Job's case. He has no real hope. The lack of an umpire and no hope of life after death show that Job is helpless before God. The Witness and the Redeemer show Job's friends that he is not alone and his case will come to court. Once the point is made, Job drops the desperate tools he used to make it. The idea that the demands of absolute justice must be met brings hopes to Job that in themselves are untenable.

Zophar can hardly wait to talk (20:2). He is being guided by a spirit (20:3). After being insulted by Job, he is ready to impart his understanding. It is interesting to note that the friends refer to wisdom outside of themselves to justify their conclusions; it is something that Job should have known all along. They are merely the agents of judgment but God is the one carrying it out. Zophar is willing to admit that at times it seems as if the wicked prosper, but it is only for a little while (20:4–5). (This is a little bit of a breakthrough for the friends.) It is only a brief interlude before disaster. Could this possibly have been Job's fate? The wicked will disappear forever (20:6–11). Mortals are necessarily stupid before God. The wicked will succumb to the self-poisoning of their own malice (20:12–15). They will not be able to enjoy the fruits of their labor (20:16–19). Notice that the charges against Job begin to get a little more specific in verse 20:19. It is interesting to compare this verse with some of the other charges (1:15; 6:4; 7:20; 16:13–14; 20:28). The wicked will be impoverished by their own greed:

> They knew no quiet in their bellies; in their greed they let nothing escape. There was nothing left after they had eaten; therefore their prosperity will not endure. In full sufficiency they will be in distress; all the force of misery will come upon them. (Job 20:20–22)

They may be able to hide their wickedness for a while but eventually it will be revealed. At that time they will lose all that they have (like Job?) (20:23–29).

For the friends and also still for Job, the cause and effect moral order represents the ideal. Under it a person would know where they stand. They would not be demoralized by good fortune nor by terror. There would be no fear or excitement in dealing with God. Righteousness can only stand in itself through man's free choice of it.

The issue being considered in chapter one is the relationship of spiritual power and honor. Truly honorable acts are done because they are right in themselves; not because they are forced by fear or because of a promise of reward. How can it be proper righteousness if it is imposed upon one? Then it would only be response to a stimulus. If a person serves God for nothing or actually in spite of everything, then they assert the sovereignty of a force that moves independent of coercion. Human integrity thus supports both sides. The dignity of persons is upheld, and the majesty of God is maintained as God's will is done without compulsion.

The question that was raised in the prologue is, "Can there be human righteousness apart from material coercion?" In the poetry the question is asked, Can God be considered just apart from His cosmic power? Does God's righteousness or honor only exist because of His control of natural forces? God has no honor if he relies on power to coerce people into divine character. If one does respond only to power, they are creatures of their own environment. God simply becomes the inescapable essence of environment. A person of formally irreproachable character may be without inward honor because the moment that they encounter what appears to be a force greater than God, they will at once alter the conduct of their life to satisfy his new master. Isn't this what has happened as science is able to explain phenomena that was previously attributed to God? This is where the old "God of the gaps" idea went wrong. Surprisingly, people are still trying to follow it today.

The only way that one may submit to the will of God as the basic source of their honor without imperiling that honor is to do so in freedom. One identifies with the right in itself and holds fast in spite of the consequences. Thus the assertion of the honor of God and that of humans is really one process. This process is simply to demonstrate that a person may retain their integrity—that is, their honor as it is within themselves—within what seems to be a disintegrating moral universe.

The Book of Job sets out, in the prologue, to show that authentic honor is a possibility for moral giants. The dialogue dares the greater task of showing how, in the grace of God, honor is a possibility for everyone.

Job thinks the reason the friends have not understood him is that they have not been paying attention. (21:2–3); so if they will just be quiet and let him finish, then they can mock him. He wants them to know that he really doesn't have a complaint with them (21:4) but with God. No wonder he is impatient. If his friends have any doubt about who is responsible for his condition, all they have to do is look at him and it will be obvious:

> Listen carefully to my words, and let this be your consolation. Bear with me, and I will speak; then after I have spoken, mock on. As for me, is my complaint addressed to mortals? Why should I not be impatient? Look at me, and be appalled, and lay your hand upon your mouth. When I think of it I am dismayed, and shuddering seizes my flesh. (Job 21:2–6)

In the passage 21:7–16 Job asks a question that a lot of people ask today, "Why do the wicked seem to get away with being evil and even prosper while many righteous people suffer?" He describes the prosperity of the wicked. You can detect that he thinks their fate (21:13, 23–24) should really have been his. A righteous person should expect this to be his treatment. In their comfortable position, evil people find no need for God (21:14–16). Do you think that many people today have this same attitude? Is the great prosperity the world is enjoying, especially in this country, causing them to forget God? Is it easier to serve God in prosperity or in poverty? Does one's status affect his devotion to God? Should it be a factor?

We saw back in chapter 18 that Bildad described the fate of the wicked. Job begins to dispute the claims the three friends are making about the prospects of the wicked. 21:17 is a direct reference to 18:5.

> How often is the lamp of the wicked put out? How often does calamity come upon them? How often does God distribute pains in his anger? (Job 21:17)

> Surely the light of the wicked is put out, and the flame of their fire does not shine. (Job 18:5)

Job wants the wicked to be punished, not their descendants (21:19–20). Job has noticed that death is a great equalizer (21:23–26). This will be a prominent theme in his speeches from here on. There is no distinguishing future for the good person or the evil person. The righteous are just as prone to suffer as the wicked.

Job accuses the three friends of scheming to wrong him (21:27). He doesn't really know why they have to take a position that he feels is against him, but he does want to make a point. He is trying to get their attention and, incidentally, the attention of God. In fact at this time, he has probably given up on ever getting a favorable response from the friends. However he still hopes to get God's attention. You will notice that a lot of Job's remaining comments seem to be directed to God. It is clear to Job that the friends have not been very observant or they would know these things (21:29–30). They have been looking at things the way they would like for them to be but not the way they actually are.

As far as Job can tell, no one ever judges the wicked (and by implication never applauds the righteous). Regardless of the way you live, you will wind up with the same fate:

> Who declares their way to their face, and who repays them for what they have done? When they are carried to the grave, a watch is kept over their tomb. The clods of the valley are sweet to them; everyone will follow after, and those who went before are innumerable. How then will you comfort me with empty nothings? There is nothing left of your answers but falsehood. (Job 21:31–34)

Job ended this speech with a vigorous denunciation of the efforts of the friends to comfort him. There has been nothing of substance in anything that they have had to say. Does this prompt the friends to take a harsher stance with him and make the attack more personal?

CHAPTER 6

The Final Round

The only thing about man that is a man . . . is his mind.
Everything else you can find in a pig or a horse.
—Archibald MacLeish

For the final attack on Job, the friends resort to personal accusations. These accusations are not true, of course. Job has given up on getting any help from the friends, so his pleas turn to the hope of getting a fair hearing, if not from the onlookers, then from God Himself. In the specific charges brought against Job, we will notice that they are the exact opposite of the way Job lived. It is interesting to compare the charges with the claims Job makes in his oath of clearance in chapters 29–31. Notice the blunt brutality of the attack.

First of all Eliphaz points out that there is no way that a mortal can be profitable to God (22:2). A person's wisdom is only of benefit to himself. Besides, God does not need our righteousness (22:3), it simply does not matter. Is this really the case? Does God get any pleasure out of our righteousness? Eliphaz does not think God ever punishes one who fears Him (22:4). And Job is obviously being punished. In a way, the friends are really optimistic, there is no question but what Job can be restored. He only has to admit his sins and confess to God. (But Job believes if he can ever present his case to God, he will be restored.)

Can a mortal be of use to God? Can even the
wisest be of service to him? Is it any pleasure to the
Almighty if you are righteous, or is it gain to him if
you make your ways blameless? Is it for your piety
that he reproves you, and enters into judgment with
you? (Job 22:2–4)

In the next passage (22:5–11) the specific charges are
leveled. The calamities that Job has suffered are great so Job's
wickedness must be great also (22:5). These sins explain why
Job's lot is worse than others. In short Job has been the worst
of sinners. However we and Job know better. Later on when
Job makes his "oath of clearance" in chapter 31, he will directly
address the falseness of the specific accusations. Compare the
following verses: 22:6 with 31:13, 19; chapter 22:7 with 31:16;
chapter 22:9 with 31:16b–18.

Perhaps, Eliphaz says, Job thought he could get away with
it because God would not see him. So Eliphaz emphasizes that
nothing could be further from the truth (22:12–20). Any really
righteous person would be able to see the punishment of the
wicked and would be glad of it (22:19–20). Whom do we know
that seem to be glad that they are witnessing the punishment
of the wicked?

One of the amazing passages that pleads for Job to repent
is in 22:21–30. Eliphaz does not say that Job should repent
of being a human. He should repent of those acts that went
beyond human error into great transgression. Job must admit
that he has been living a lie and sue for mercy. (The fact that
Job does not see his sins is of little importance.) But for Job
to accept forgiveness would be further dishonor, the insult of
being forgiven by one's offender.

If one removed verses 24 and 25, this would make a great
invitation after one of our present-day sermons. Perhaps the
impact is not great upon people because they, like Job, do not
feel that they have been great sinners. The realizations of this
should help in our reaching people, and temper the way we
present the gospel.

The obsession Job has of finding God and laying his case before Him grows. It is really hard to defend yourself if you don't even know where the court is and the judge does not appear. Job admits to being bitter because his complaint has not been heard (23:2) and God deals him a heavy hand. Zophar had already told Job in 11:7–8 that God was inscrutable. Job thinks that he has a very good case; all he has to do is present it. He momentarily believes it would be a fair trial.

> I would lay my case before him, and fill my mouth with arguments. I would learn what he would answer me, and understand what he would say to me. Would he contend with me in the greatness of his power? No; but he would give heed to me. There an upright person could reason with him, and I should be acquitted forever by my judge. (Job 23:4–7)

This is perhaps the most significant of all of Job's statements of hope. God would not render him speechless and confuse him. A little more confidence is shown here than back in chapter 9 (verses 3, 15, 19, 20, 32, 34–35).

But, alas, Job cannot find the way. He has searched everywhere for God, but has not found him (23:8–9). Some overzealous preachers have made a big deal of the fact that Job does not say he looked up, claiming that is the only place to find God. Such assertions miss the point of his search. He has been searching in the realm that he and his friends always believed to be where God operated, in the sphere of their own experience. When God does appear in chapter 38, it is out of the whirlwind described by Elihu, and not from above. Job thinks he will be found innocent in the day of the trial (23:10) because he has held to God's ways (23:11–12). However, God has become strange and unfamiliar, which causes Job to be afraid.

> But he stands alone and who can dissuade him? What he desires, that he does. For he will complete what he appoints for me; and many such things are in his mind. Therefore I am terrified at his presence; when I consider, I am in dread of him. God has made

> my heart faint; the Almighty has terrified me; if only
> I could vanish in darkness, and thick darkness would
> cover my face! (Job 23:13–17)

A fair hearing is all Job wants. He seems to be developing a new confidence. The theme that began in chapter 21 is expanded upon in chapter 24. The whole of the chapter shows the injustices tolerated by God. He may even be responsible for some of them. It is shown that many wicked are not punished. Many poor suffer at the hands of their fellow beings. In spite of that, God still does not hear their prayers (24:12). The friends are saying those who rebel against God are swiftly punished. Instead the powerful are supported. Job challenges them to show that he is wrong (24:25).

At first this would seem to be a discouragement to Job. Far from it. By the examples he has cited, Job's own case is strengthened. He now has the testimony of others to add to his own. History shows many examples of God's injustice if one only looks for them. In addition many outrages are perpetuated by people upon one another. Job rests his case outside himself because it can readily be seen in the common experience of humanity.

Job has found human companionship; he plundered, and the persecuted, the ravished are everywhere. He is their self-appointed spokesman at the judgment bar. It is pleasant to get satisfaction for your own complaints while pleading for another. You can vehemently proclaim the injustice of a law a lot more sincerely after you have received your own summons. Significantly, Job did not approach God about victimized humanity until he became a victim.

Job's confidence is conditional. He is obsessed with justice. It has become a fundamental preoccupation. He has been just, but has been unjustly treated. His highest hopes are to arrange a confrontation with God so that the truth will appear. This will form the blueprint for his restoration. He wants relief to make reconciliation possible, and to be able to experience it. He is not interested in the return of creature comforts for their own sake.

Is Job just being a good psychologist here? Is he merely polishing the apple? We can compare this to Hezekiah's approach (Isaiah 38:16–19). If Hezekiah is spared, fifteen more years of praises will rise to God. But Hezekiah will enjoy good things too. A cynic might think that Job is really only interested the perquisites that go with reconciliation.

CHAPTER 7

The Problems with the Text

*The dissenter is every human being at those moments of his
life when he resigns momentarily from the herd and thinks
for himself.*

—Archibald MacLeish

This section of the book presents some textual problems (chapters 25–28). Every commentator will address these problems. The solutions that are offered are many and varied, even at times contradictory. The resolution of the problems is not essential to gaining the great lessons the book has to offer and do not detract from it in any way. Because no new insights appear, the problem passages should not concern the reader. Only passing reference will be made to some of the solutions that have been proposed.

The problems are these: The speech of Bildad in chapter 25 is very short, only six verses and he addresses just one topic briefly. The symmetry of the poetry is broken by not having a third speech of Zophar. Chapter 27:13–23 is in a speech attributed to Job, but the discussion sounds exactly like the arguments of the three friends. The miserable fate of the wicked is described. The passage thus could be a continuation of Bildad's comments, or it could be the missing speech of Zophar. It could also be Job mocking or parroting his friends. Chapter 28 (which is still in the speech of Job) is a great discourse on wisdom that has no ties to what comes before or after. That does not positively prove that Job did not utter it. In it mortals have no wisdom of their own. Wisdom is worth more than anything else (28:12–19). Only God knows the way to it (28:23). The fear of the Lord is wisdom (28:28). We will treat the text as we have it.

The summation given by Bildad focuses on the vast differences between God and humans. Dominion and fear are with God (25:2–3). It is He who makes peace even though He is in heaven. His armies are overwhelming. He provides the light to all.

Because of the great majesty that God has, it is impossible for any person to be righteous before Him (25:4–6). (When we focus on the majesty of God, do we impart the same impression?) Mortals are unclean basically, inescapably so. Compare this passage with chapter 15:14–16 and chapter 22:2–3. Humans are simply on a plane with the worms. Bildad is not disturbed by the prospect of one's ultimately joining the worms. He sums up the spirit of the friends' discourses which were started in chapter 4:17–19. It was easy for Bildad to speak of a human as a worm; but Job, nearest of all to that level, will not say mother to a maggot.

Job begins by recounting how the friends have helped him (26:2–3). I love the great sarcasm. They have provided power and strength, of course not! Knowledge and wisdom have flowed from their lips, of course not! Their comforting and consoling capability have been so bad that Job wonders whom they really represent (26:4).

Just to show that he knows as much as they, Job describes how God's power is always manifest (26:5–14). God has control of the heavens. The sea can be stilled by Him. Even the places hidden from human view are open to Him. The things mentioned are but a touch of His power. He is beyond any force. (As a digression, I do not believe that 26:7 is a prescience statement. It is merely a description from the view available to Job.)

Job refuses to retreat from his position (27:1–6). Notice that in this passage the issue is still not the existence of God (as happens when people suffer unjustly today), but rather the changed nature of God as He deals with Job now. Job will never relinquish his integrity (27:5). In reviewing his life, he has found no reason for reproach. He will never admit that the friends are right.

The issue is clearly joined. The honor of Job as a representative citizen of a moral universe has been stained. What has happened is a violation of his nature; he is the victim of God. The violence done was external, but its real impact is within (and so with us today). Job is under personal attack. His only defense is his integrity.

The suffering of Job is so intense that he will exaggerate to strengthen his case as he whimpers for relief from distress. He excuses it due to his suffering (6:26; 9:34–35). The case he has presented is irrefutable. It has been constructed on careful portrayal of the situation in which he finds himself and resulted in a forceful argument. His ultimate goal is vindication and restoration.

Humans have always had spiritual yearnings (every culture has had some sort of worship). A cynic might miss seeing this fact. Satan certainly missed seeing it the prologue. Man does not live by bread alone and is never really satisfied with it. He asks why he is here, what purpose produced him, and to what end? However they live, humans endlessly seek a frame of reference in which they cannot bear themselves except as a spiritual identity.

We can see different motives in Job's request for God to remove the sufferings. The physical pain was real while the spiritual part of him wonders about man's existence. Job is intensely human, speaking to and for the race.

Job has shown no weakening under the barrage from the friends, rather he has gained strength. He has not caved in due to the negative opinions expressed by the friends; rather, his determination has been enhanced and his resolve strengthened. He has silenced the friends and is ready to tell God to "step outside and say that." Job is not on trial; God is! This will help to understand the tone of God's speech. If God does not appear, Job will be the victor. If God does appear, Job is certain that he will be vindicated. At last God is caught in the either/or situation that has given people their worst moments. Again and again Everyman has found himself trapped in the unyielding arms of moral law.

CHAPTER 8

Wisdom

*We have learned the answers, all the answers: it is the question
that we do not know.*
—Archibald MacLeish

There is a genre of ancient literature known collectively as
wisdom literature. Every culture had its own version in
which rules of conduct were expressed. These rules ranged from
individual thought to social interactions and intended to be
practical in application. In the Bible five books are considered
to be wisdom literature: Job, Psalms, Proverbs, Ecclesiastes,
and Song of Solomon. It is not clear if there is a modern example; probably not that found on the opinion/editorial pages of
newspapers or posts on Twitter. Some would place Benjamin
Franklin's *Poor Richard's Almanac* in that category.

It has been noted earlier that chapter 28 presents struc-
tural problems in the Book of Job. There is no introduction
telling us for certain who the speaker is. It is often assumed
that because Job was identified as the speaker in 27:1 that he
continues through chapter 31. However 27:1 and 29:1 both
begin with "Job again took up discourse," indicating a break
in Job's speech somewhere in between. The gap is thought to
be filled with two parts, 27:7–23 being a presumed missing last
speech of Zophar or one of the other friends and chapter 28
being supplied by someone else. In such a scenario chapter 28
is ascribed to the narrator of chapters 1, 2, and 42 and would

violate no cause for it all being the word of God nor detract anything from the message. One's opinion would depend on how one views inspiration of the Bible. To those who hold to a literal, word-for-word style of inspiration, this would not be allowed. Word for word would only be for the original language, in this case Hebrew. Does this mean that the same word for word applies to translation into other languages? English is such a dynamic, ever-changing language that inspiration would have to extend over many incarnations of it (and also for many other languages). Perhaps that is why some accept only one translation as the true word of God in English. Unfortunately over time many English words change their meaning. Then the question arises about Scripture, such as some of the Psalms which offer praise to God. Did God dictate His own praise? I have to accept the position that the word as we have it is what God intended us to have by whatever means.

Notice the very negative attitude by Job in 27:2–6:

> As God lives, who has taken away my right, and the Almighty, who has made my soul bitter, as long as my breath is in me and the spirit of God is in my nostrils, my lips will not speak falsehood, and my tongue will not utter deceit. Far be it from me to say that you are right; until I die I will not put away my integrity from me. I hold fast my righteousness, and will not let it go; my heart does not reproach me for any of my days.

Job has used similar language throughout the dialogue. The friends have also been negative in their assessment of Job's condition. We will see later that the as yet unknown observer, Elihu, will also persist in negativism. In so doing the concepts of wisdom and being wise are often raised to justify their positions. The discourse on wisdom fits very well as a transition between negativism and the speech of God. If it were directly between the speech of Elihu and that of God, perhaps the transitional position would be clearer. But the chapter is included in our Scripture and has some purpose so should be studied in spite our lack of wisdom about it. Job, Eliphaz, Bildad, and Zophar have been citing wisdom all along and Elihu will do so later. Therefore it should be important to understand what wisdom is and what it is all about.

First we can look at how each of the characters considered wisdom and being wise applied to them by tracing their thoughts.

Eliphaz first establishes his credentials for being able to expound on wisdom:

> Now a word came stealing to me, my ear received the whisper of it. Amid thoughts from visions of the night, when deep sleep falls on mortals, dread came upon me, and trembling, A spirit glided past my face; the hair of my flesh bristled. It stood still, but I could not discern its appearance. A form was before my eyes; there was silence, then I heard a voice. (Job 4:12–16)

He and Bildad and Zophar have done extensive research on problems similar to Job's that he can learn from.

> See, we have searched this out; it is true. Hear, and know it for yourself. (Job 5:27)

Others have access to wisdom based upon their experience gained over time. They are not merely speaking for themselves; they are the voice of God!

> Have you listened in the council of God? And do you limit wisdom to yourself? What do you know that we do not know? What do you understand that is not clear to us? The gray-haired and the aged are on our side, those older than your father. Are the consolations of God too small for you, or the word that deals gently with you? (Job 15:8–11)

> I will show you; listen to me; what I have seen I will declare—what sages have told, and their ancestors have not hidden. (Job 15:17–18)

Mortals are so far inferior to God that they are subjected to God's judgment because they have not wisdom.

> Their tent-cord is plucked up within them, and they die devoid of wisdom. (Job 4:21)

Bildad also appeals to the wisdom of their fathers because Job and his contemporaries' experiences are so limited.

> For inquire now of bygone generations, and consider what their ancestors have found; for we are but of yesterday, and we know nothing, for our days on earth are but a shadow. Will they not teach you and tell you and utter words out of their understanding? (Job 8:8–10)

For Job to ignore the wisdom of the ages is to expect the whole order of things to be overturned just to accommodate him (18:2–4).

> How long will you hunt for words? Consider, and then we shall speak. Why are we counted as cattle? Why are we stupid in your sight? You who tear yourself in your anger—shall the earth be forsaken because of you, or the rock be removed out of its place? (Job 18:2–4)

Zophar is sure that Job is talking nonsense and if it is properly exposed, others will be able to answer him; he should be ashamed of himself, especially for his mocking of those who are trying to help. Job needs for God to set him straight.

> Should a multitude of words go unanswered, and should one full of talk be vindicated? Should your babble put others to silence, and when you mock, shall no one shame you? For you say, 'My conduct is pure, and I am clean in God's sight.' But O that God would speak, and open his lips to you, and that he would tell you the secrets of wisdom! For wisdom is many-sided. (Job 11:2–6)

The gist of the three friends' arguments is based on precedents from the past. What they are saying has been believed by everyone for a long time. Wisdom comes from age, engaged in careful observation which makes it equivalent to the wisdom of God for whom they are speaking.

When Job finalizes his defense summed up in his "oath of clearance" in chapters 29–31, a new voice appears on the scene. His views will be dealt with later but it is interesting at this point note his evaluation on the wisdom and its source presented by the three friends (32:6–13).

> Elihu son of Barachel the Buzite answered: "I am young in years, and you are aged; therefore I was timid and afraid to declare my opinion to you. I said, 'Let days speak, and many years teach wisdom.' But truly it is the spirit in a mortal, the breath of the Almighty, that makes for understanding. It is not the old that are wise, nor the aged that understand what is right. Therefore I say, 'Listen to me; let me also declare my opinion.' See, I waited for your words, I listened for your wise sayings, while you searched out what to say. I gave you my attention, but there was in fact no one that confuted Job, no one among you that answered his words. Yet do not say, 'We have found wisdom; God may vanquish him, not a human.'" (Job 32:6–13)

Thus all of the principles in the story have claimed to be a receptacle of wisdom gained through various types of experiences. Job refuses to accept their conclusions and admit that he has been in the wrong. To do so would be a violation of his integrity; he will not confess something that is not true and become a false witness. With all of this emphasis on wisdom, it would be appropriate to include a discussion of the subject.

People have always looked for treasure and expended great effort to obtain it (28:1–11). The treasures they sought were of a material nature. The examples given in this passage are those related to mining precious metals and gems. Mining has always required hard work, especially in those times, but people were willing to take the risks even though a reward was not always obtained. History contains many accounts of miners enduring hardships and dangers in various gold rushes and the like. Very few actually "struck it rich." Although the costs are not as great, people express the same hope today by entering lotteries where the odds of winning are diminishingly small. The birds and beasts are not tempted by the desire for treasure like people are.

There is a much more valuable treasure to be had in wisdom but it requires a different method of prospecting (28:12–19). It is more highly prized than those treasures normally sought. It also has a different source and is harder to find than material treasures (28:20–22). God is the only one who understands where it dwells and how to get to it (28:23). In the somewhat cryptic passage that ends the chapter; the way to wisdom is available to anyone who observes closely enough. It is seen in all of creation which was the work of God. Wisdom and understanding are then easily obtained:

> And he said to humankind, "Truly, the fear of the Lord, that is wisdom; and to depart from evil is understanding." (Job 28:28)

We can compare this to that given in Psalms and Proverbs:

> The fear of the Lord is the beginning of wisdom; all those who practice it have a good understanding. (Psalms 111:10)

> The fear of the Lord is the beginning of knowledge; fools despise wisdom and instruction. (Proverbs 1:7)

> The fear of the Lord is the beginning of wisdom, and the knowledge of the Holy One is insight. (Proverbs 9:10)

In these last three verses, the fear of the Lord is only the beginning while in Job it is stated stronger. Fear, as used there and many other Old Testament passages, is not in the sense of abject terror but in the sense of respect. The Hebrew word is *yirah* which carries the meaning of reverence and awe. For us it means wonder and gratitude for all God has created and all he has done for us. It is possible to have knowledge without understanding because we do not know the implications of that knowledge. It is possible to have understanding without wisdom because we do not put it into practice. People who have all three are rare; but we expect that of those in whom we put our trust. This would include our mentors, teachers, family, religious leaders, civil leaders, and other esteemed individuals. Thus we put a larger burden on them than we do ourselves. We must recognize the order; we cannot have wisdom without understanding, and we cannot have understanding without knowledge. Eliphaz, Bildad, Zophar, and Elihu all tried to radiate wisdom when they did not have the knowledge. Thus they suffered God's rebuke.

CHAPTER 9

Discourse: Job's Closing Arguments

Man depends on God for all things: God depends on man for one. Without man's love God does not exist as God, only creator, and love is the one thing no one, not even God Himself can command.

—Archibald MacLeish

It is interesting to review chapter three and compare Job's attitude there with his attitude now. He has changed his position about what he wants to happen. In chapter three he was hoping for death, now he wants life and restoration. And he is willing to fight for it. Apparently the change happened because Job saw in the friends' arguments that his honor would be forever tarnished if vindication were not accomplished before he died. One wonders whether he would have ever reached this conclusion if the friends had merely offered him pity as he desired. There ought to be a lesson there for us in how we deal with suffering people (it may well be different for different personalities). Do we simply offer pity, or do we admonish? How do we avoid alienating them? We should never condemn, belittle, or otherwise show disregard for the depths of their anguish.

In the old days Job knew that God watched over him and was always with him (29:2–6). These are the days to which he wishes to return. But now God is gone, and didn't even leave a note. Job was held in high esteem and honor by his community (29:7–11, 25). They honored him with good reason. Job had been rich, but for philanthropic reasons. He had provided for the needy, he had been a one-man welfare department (29:12–17). In everything he had been just (29:14). The loss of status might not have stung so much if people had not used it as an occasion against Job. The loss seemed to be emphasized by those who daunted him, especially because they had had a much lower status than he. Thus we see mortals carrying out what they believe to be the just judgments of God. So for Job the equality of Sheol is not good enough. There are some that deserve no respect, his pride shows.

> But now they make sport of me, those who are younger than I, whose fathers I would have disdained to set with the dogs of my flock. What could I gain from the strength of their hands? All their vigor is gone. Through want and hard hunger they gnaw the dry and desolate ground they pick mallow and the leaves of bushes, and to warm themselves the roots of broom. They are driven out from society; people shout after them as after a thief. In the gullies of wadis they must live, in holes in the ground, and in the rocks. Among the bushes they bray; under the nettles they huddle together. A senseless, disreputable brood, they have been whipped out of the land. (Job 30:1–8)

Those who are sub-human make sport of Job (30:9–15). Job must present them as starkly as possible so the scandal of his case may be perfectly clear. Of the things that are missing Job lists two. His honor is gone (listed first) and his prosperity has dissipated (30:15).

Because only God has such great power, Job constantly reminds the audience that his condition is from God (30:16–23). He does not let the spectator forget what an unbelievable parody of humanity he has become. Job has constantly asked for help but received no answer (30:20). Death remains as his only prospect.

> I know that you will bring me to death, and to the
> house appointed for all living. (Job 30:23)

All the torments strike at Job's honor. That was Satan's challenge in 1:9. Job does not deny God's right to assign affliction to dishonorable men. He continues to believe that the betrayal of moral law merits grievous punishment. What he refuses to accept is the violent disgrace of a man by forces beyond his control.

At the beginning of the book, Job was not told what the issue was, he is never told, and he doesn't figure it out. Thus in his mind he conceives, does God subject himself to the same standards he has placed on mortals? If not, God must explain why. Job has become the poster child of all God's misdeeds. Job is a very unlikely standard bearer; he is near death and rejected by all he knows:

> He has put my family far from me, and my acquaintances are wholly estranged from me. My relatives and my close friends have failed me; the guests in my house have forgotten me; my serving girls count me as a stranger; I have become an alien in their eyes. I call to my servant, but he gives me no answer; I must myself plead with him. My breath is repulsive to my wife; I am loathsome to my own family. Even young children despise me; when I rise, they talk against me. All my intimate friends abhor me, and those whom I loved have turned against me. (Job 19:13–19)

One in Job's condition hardly represents much of a threat to God. His weapon is not of power or might but challenging the honor of God; it is a weapon no one else has. Thus the honor of God is also at stake for His indefensible outrage against Job. God can no longer place His failures on human shoulders, for Job's experience testifies otherwise. God is granted one of two alternatives: either He must restore Job to prosperity or prove that Job was in the wrong. Job asks that he get precisely what he deserves; the restoration of the old, happy order of things.

Not only is Job suffering from pain, which is hard to bear in itself, but he must suffer the indignity of his loss of status. He has joined the ranks of all those who experience similar indignities; the senile, the cripples, the beggars, the handicapped, the homeless, and others looked down upon by society. It does not matter if one tries to have sympathy and say, "But it is not their fault," which is both true and irrelevant. You simply cannot argue with a condition.

The code expressed by Job in chapter 31 and executed in his life is predominately moral, appealing to conscience and highlighting the inner man. Job does not make the mistake of citing formal piety. Job has always had the welfare of others in mind. He has not assaulted the honor of his neighbor's wife (31:1-2). He has not despised the cause of his servants (31:13-15). He has not neglected the needs of the poor (31:16-21). He has not secretly worshiped others (31:24-27). Nor has he ever been hypocritical (31:33-34). He has even dealt faithfully with his land (31:38-39). Job asserts his dignity as a citizen of a world of honor. He will take the indictment of his adversary and display it for all to see. He refuses to accept either the stigma of his human smallness or responsibility for the extraordinary sins he is accused of committing.

Job's good deeds express honor, not the requirements of statutes! He considered women honorably (31:1,9). He sustained the worth of slaves (31:13). He cared for the helpless and poor (31:16-31). He did not seek reassurance from wealth or the sun or the moon (31:25-26). He has not rejoiced in the ruin of his enemies (31:29).

Job presents challenges to God. Job wants God to come out into the open (31:35). (Compare with Hebrews 12:22-24.) Job will approach him like a prince (31:37) not as a worm (25:6). This is Job's final summons to God. God has not dealt faithfully with his world like Job has done with his. Job would not have allowed injustice to a good man. From the standpoint of phenomenal power, God is still on the throne, He is in no jeopardy. But from the standpoint of the immovable realities of right and wrong, heaven is under serious attack.

Job has discovered that God really is God. This discovery is by no means new, it first occurred in Eden. Subsequently the whole race has paused at the forbidden tree, seeking a shortcut to divinity. That Job takes the seat of majesty should not surprise us, for by now we should know who Job is. Job is mankind.

It is worth repeating at this time a point from earlier. Job represents all those whose experience violates a faith once held. Words and dogmas, satisfactory for solving theoretical problems, may actually intensify personal crisis. The extraordinary predicament of Job is not intended to lift him out of the experience or ordinary people. His catastrophes simply represent in the objective world that which occurs subjectively in one's own universe when tragedy strikes.

CHAPTER 10

Discourse: Elihu, the Strident Voice of Angry Youth

You wanted justice, didn't you? There isn't any . . . there is only love.
—Archibald MacLeish, J. B.'s wife in *J. B.*

E lihu is somewhat of an enigma. All we know about him is contained in these chapters. Yet he speaks more than the three friends do. No doubt there were spectators to the debate and he was one of the crowd. He is ignored by everyone. Some think he may have been a later addition by some Rabbi trying to make the book fit Jewish tradition. Elihu's arguments are probably what we would think today and, indeed, one often hears them. According to the response of God, Elihu's arguments are of no more value than those of the other three friends are. Therefore, bear in mind when we discuss the arguments of Elihu, we are only trying to understand his logic; not recommending his opinions. When God speaks, it as if Elihu had never been present. God neither endorses nor condemns what Elihu has said. He will denounce what the other three have said and praise Job. The analysis is not to be construed as sound advice for us but do give a useful insight into some Jewish thought of the time.

First of all notice why the three ceased their arguing (32:1). Then notice why Elihu feels compelled to answer Job and why he has waited (just like today, huh?) (32:2–4). Job's arguments were unanswerable by a human. Certainly the three friends did not answer him (32:3). In fact, only God can properly answer Job (a fact Job has been maintaining all along) (32:13). However this does not keep Elihu from trying because he is in a unique position; sort of a disinterested observer or friend of the court:

> Elihu son of Barachel the Buzite answered: "I am young in years, and you are aged; therefore I was timid and afraid to declare my opinion to you. I said, 'Let days speak, and many years teach wisdom.' But truly it is the spirit in a mortal, the breath of the Almighty, that makes for understanding. It is not the old that are wise, nor the aged that understand what is right. Therefore I say, 'Listen to me; let me also declare my opinion.'" (Job 32:6–10)

Elihu feels he must speak because the weakness of Job's position may be exposed by proper arguments. Elihu has suffered through the debate (32:19). Throughout chapters 32 and 33, Elihu keeps saying he is about to say something without ever really getting it said. Typical of youth, his mind is clear because it is uncluttered with information.

Elihu considers himself peculiarly able to help Job. He intends to draw the truth of God out of the realm of the intuitional, where one grasps at the unspoken or hinted purposes of God. Elihu is not burdened with the past or its misconceptions (32:9). Today's truth is not to be found in the epigrams of an idealized past. Elihu has been given a gift from God (32:8, 18; 33:3–4). He brings no new information to Job; he merely interprets events that are common to the experience of people. All people have access to God the same as Elihu if they rightly search for God (32:8; 33:4). Elihu really refers to the rational capacity of humans. He feels he always has access to the sublime inward certainties of the rational mind. A human's glory is to know; God's glory is to reveal. Job had asked for a mediator (9:33), and Elihu can be sympathetic to mortals (33:6–7).

Elihu describes the function of a mediator (33:19–28). In so doing he may be referring to himself. He thinks highly of his ability to interpret God. God speaks in ways a mortal does not understand (33:14–15). If dreams fail, God speaks through suffering so Job must listen (33:31–33). Elihu never mentions the method of restoration. This is not his business. He does say what is good for humans (33:23). Elihu almost suggests a sacramental procedure (33:26–27), yet his whole intent is to study the ways of God with people outside formal religion. Elihu's mediator is not the one Job desires. Elihu maintains God is beyond law. He emphasizes that God reveals things to people, even if He has to do it through suffering.

God is not capricious or arbitrary. A clear mind sees that the works of God are just. Only confused thinking would put it otherwise. God governs the universe; He is responsible for the world (34:13–15). So how could God hate justice (34:17–19)? He merely shows no respect for human pretensions; it is God's proper estate. Finally death comes to all (34:20).

> Shall one who hates justice govern? Will you condemn one who is righteous and mighty, who says to a king, "You scoundrel!" and to princes, "You wicked men!"; who shows no partiality to nobles, nor regards the rich more than the poor, for they are all the work of his hands? In a moment they die; at midnight the people are shaken and pass away, and the mighty are taken away by no human hand. (Job 34:17–20)

God is not moved by what we would call "personal" reasons. Wickedness does not affect Him (35:6). Righteousness does not profit Him (35:7). A person's actions have consequences for themselves alone (35:8). God's might makes right; it guarantees his justice. It puts Him beyond fear and selfishness. This is the opposite of Job's arguments in chapter 9. Elihu is more of a retributionist than the three friends. However he does not accuse Job of sin. He just points out that affliction is God's way of talking to Job. The difference in Elihu's approach is in the use of "by" (36:15). There is a process working within human experience that saves him. God is working in Job and has called for Job in the terrible urgency of pain.

God is in the order of things, which illustrates how catastrophe relates to providence. Storms both judge (36:33) and give food (36:31). Thus storms accomplish different things for God (37:12–13). The lightening of God's anger opens up the rain clouds of His mercy. The afflicted receive their right (36:6). The righteous are sometimes afflicted (36:7–9) and sometimes they afflict themselves. Too often the favor of God is misconstrued as favoritism. Only by withdrawing favor can God overcome arrogance.

Affliction becomes a way to correct humans. If one repents then they are restored (36:11). If one does not hearken, then they are punished (36:12). Being blessed or cursed is up to the sufferer (36:18). Punishment may turn out to be a ransom; the greater the suffering, the greater the blessing. Some people may revile God because of their suffering (36:13). In contrast, outrage never saved anybody (35:10–11). There is actually a dignity in suffering. God does not speak to His other creatures this way.

Elihu claims that Job has refused to listen to God. Humans are equipped to know God. Therefore, Job's ignorance is willful. Job has attempted the impossibility of negotiating with an impartial God:

> There they cry out, but he does not answer, because of the pride of evildoers. Surely God does not hear an empty cry, nor does the Almighty regard it. How much less when you say that you do not see him, that the case is before him, and you are waiting for him! (Job 35:12–14)

By so doing Job is an ally of the hopelessly wicked (36:17–18). Job's strength will not save him (36:19). Job has simply made the wrong choice (36:21). Whether the affliction becomes corrosive depends upon how one receives it. Pain and sorrow represent new opportunities in the wise (good) person for the soul's inquiry toward the will of God.

Elihu uses the term "pit" instead of "Sheol" (the NIV uses "death" instead of the Hebrew word "Sheol"; other version simply transliterate). Other passages to examine for the usage are 33:28, 30; Psalms 36:6; 49:15, 19; Isaiah 26:19. The terrors of the pit await the wicked. The terrors are intended to convert people (33:13–17). Humans can avoid death (33:18). The sufferer is brought close to the pit (33:22).

The enlightened one is delivered (33:24). He becomes young again (33:25) and goes into the presence of God (33:26). After they are redeemed, one testifies of salvation (33:28). Life and light are the opposite of the pit (32:28–30). Life is to be gained (33:29–30). Elihu does not use it as a lever, but hints at it (35:11; 36:20; 33:23ff).

Elihu's discussion in chapter 33 comes close to positing an existence of a life after death with a different fate for the righteous and the wicked. It is only hinted at and the subject is not pursued. This may be the beginnings of the clear distinctions between heaven and hell that are found in the New Testament. The Jewish theology was not fully developed in New Testament times as evidenced by the disputes between the Pharisees and the Sadducees over the resurrection. The Jews would have had to have some inkling of a distinction after death by what happened, first to Enoch in Genesis 5:24 and then to Elijah in 2 Kings 2:11. Elihu does not elaborate but it should have offered some hope and comfort to Job. Any case for an afterlife that could be suggested by Elihu's oratory would be very tenuous.

Elihu is concerned with defending the honor of God, not humans. He attempts to show that God's force is moral and just and that He is impartial. Humans determine whether God is a judge or a savior. What might have been a ransom becomes an execution. God bestows upon a person what a person makes themselves a candidate for. The fundamental sin of humans is pride, which may harden into arrogance and rebellion. Mortals must not remain ignorant (34:35–36). Only humanity knows God as a teacher. Enlightened humility allows one to find that God is love, after all.

In very graphic language, chapter 37 describes the approaching storm out of which God will speak:

> At this also my heart trembles, and leaps out of its place. Listen, listen to the thunder of his voice and the rumbling that comes from his mouth. Under the whole heaven he lets it loose, and his lightning to the corners of the earth. After it his voice roars; he thunders with his majestic voice and he does not restrain the lightning when his voice is heard. God thunders wondrously with his voice; he does great things that we cannot comprehend. For to the snow he says, 'Fall on the earth'; and the shower of rain, his heavy shower of rain, serves as a sign on everyone's hand, so that all whom he has made may know it. Then the animals go into their lairs and remain in their dens. From its chamber comes the whirlwind, and cold from the scattering winds. By the breath of God ice is given, and the broad waters are frozen fast. He loads the thick cloud with moisture; the clouds scatter his lightning. They turn round and round by his guidance, to accomplish all that he commands them on the face of the habitable world. Whether for correction, or for his land, or for love, he causes it to happen. (Job 37:1–13)

In other words, God is in control of the natural forces; they can be for good or for harm. They affect both the righteous and the wicked the same way; no distinction is made. Even animals recognize the power of nature in God's hands and respond to it. Humans should know this because of the intellect they were given by being made in the image of God. Job has no excuse for not getting the message. He can consider the wondrous works, but he cannot duplicate them. Job is not in God's league.

> The Almighty—we cannot find him; he is great in power and justice, and abundant righteousness he will not violate. Therefore mortals fear him; he does not regard any who are wise in their own conceit. (Job 37:23–24)

To many readers, probably most, Elihu's analysis makes sense; certainly more than the other three. He has not tried to examine Job's life in detail and draw conclusions based on those conclusions. He has expressed a general communication of God with people of which Job is an excellent example. All people in their stubbornness refuse to be receptive to God's messages. Sometimes God has to take drastic measures to get their attention, but, for the hearer, the effort is well worth it.

Whether Elihu has said all he wants to say is not really known. It seems he is really just getting wound up and could go on for a while longer. Some translations indicate that God actually interrupts Elihu. Whatever the case we can eagerly anticipate God's appearance.

CHAPTER 11

Discourse: God, from the Center of the Storm

What is wrong is not the great discoveries of science—information is always better than ignorance, no matter what information or what ignorance. What is wrong is the belief behind the information, the belief that information will change the world. It won't.

—Archibald MacLeish

Job has eloquently presented closing arguments for his case in chapters 29 to 31. That he has satisfactorily refuted the accusations of the three friends, or at least convinced them that no further arguments would be fruitful is indicated.

> So these three men ceased to answer Job, because he was righteous in his own eyes. (Job 32:1)

Not only were the friends convinced that further debate was futile, for Job the feeling is mutual; he can get no help from them. He is sure that he knows the source of his troubles and is ready to confront his accuser. He has resorted to directing his pleas to God when the friends were no help but has received no reply. He certainly was convinced that his case was air-tight and he was ready to present it. All he needed was to get his day in court and he would be vindicated; along with it, he will be restored to his former glory.

> O that I had one to hear me! (Here is my signa-
> ture! Let the Almighty answer me!) O, that I had the
> indictment written by my adversary! Surely I would
> carry it on my shoulder; I would bind it on me like a
> crown; I would give him an account of all my steps;
> like a prince I would approach him. (Job 31:1)

The question Satan had proposed in the prologue was whether Job was only serving God for what he could get out it; if it were all taken away, would he curse or not curse God? Does Job really have free will, or is he simply responding to the inducements God provides? In the prologue after each of the two tests, he blessed God. In the poetry, however, after cursing the day he was born, he takes a third approach. He is sure some mistake has been made and he is the victim of it. Satan's charge is such that, God cannot come to Job without invalidating the test because Job would know that God was still with him. God could certainly not hint at the reasons for Job's troubles. Even at the end when God does answer Job, it is neither to comfort him nor explain why he has been subjected to such torments, but to confront him. God chose neither of the alternatives Job had suggested: prove that Job has sinned or restore him to his proper place. The voice coming out of the whirlwind (an F-1 tornado?) that Elihu had been describing would have had to be awesome. It gives rise to the longest and most profound speech attributed entirely to God. (The long detailed instructions and laws given to Moses in Exodus, Leviticus, and Deuteronomy were not a speech.)

The nature of God's message to Job must have been quite a shock to him; his arguments seem to be ignored. It is also quite a shock to the readers. Has God changed His opinion of Job? Does He think that Satan was right after all? It is important to notice what God does not say in his encounter with Job. He does not negate any of Job's virtues; Job has remained blame-less, upright, not turned from fear of God, and continues to turn away from evil. Nowhere in the dialogue with the friends has he ever violated any of these virtues. The fault that God finds with Job is something else. How did Job "darken council without knowledge"? That will be explained by testing Job's knowledge of God's operation by a series of questions. When Job's answer is noncommittal, God continues quizzing him concerning the mythical creatures of chaos. These creatures will be treated later. Throughout the dialogue the friends have assumed the role of God; even Job at times has sought to play God. It is probable that God cannot possibly explain in clear details His working in human affairs. Both Job and the friends have admitted that, compared to God, mortals are next to nothing. As a voice from the whirlwind, God remains a mystery. This is true through all ages as Paul mentions in his writings; the most significant mystery is God's gift of Christ (Colossians 2:2, for example). It is up to God first of all to be God. "So to be" means, among other things, that God does not commit Himself to nostrums and doctrines which, while they medicate and explain, are always in competition with other medications and explanations. God does not enter directly into the argument regarding his justice to humans.

God's speech does not really violate the principle of his absence from Job. If anything, the phenomenal distance between God and humanity is increased (38:2–4). The whole speech reveals nothing of God's care for people, of the possibility of restoration, nor of hidden purposes working through human trials. Most of it is, form the standpoint of logical debate, a sublime irrelevance or perhaps not. At the end of the catastrophes we are told that Job "did not sin with his lips" (2:10). At the end of the dialogue and the beginning of God's discourse that is modified:

> Who is this that darkens counsel by words without
> knowledge? (Job 38:2)

The word *counsel* in this verse may cause confusion because of the way it is used today; it generally means advice and why a lawyer is sometimes called a counselor. The New English Bible translates this verse "Who is this whose ignorant words cloud my design in darkness?" Used in this sense, God is asking who is obscuring my plan because they lack knowledge. He is implying that He had had a plan all along but Job does not understand it. A part of that plan is that humanity (and God) has free will and is not constrained by some rigid system. The development of Job's arguments is such that God is on trial not Job. In some sense that may actually be true. We assume that Satan's challenge to God was a test of Job's faith. Did Job have unconditional faith in God? In addition, does God have faith in Job? Apparently He does to the extent that He lets Satan test Job. Would God have that much faith in each of us? Would He have asked of Satan "Have you considered my servant, [put your own name in here]?" How would God describe your character to Satan? When we suffer and are tormented, is it because God has faith in us that we will prevail? We are not promised freedom from suffering, rather we are told to expect it.

> In this you rejoice, even if now for a little while you have had to suffer various trials, so that the genuineness of your faith—being more precious than gold that, though perishable, is tested by fire—may be found to result in praise and glory and honor when Jesus Christ is revealed. (Peter 1:6–7)

This does not make the suffering any easier; otherwise it would not be suffering. This is also easy to say if I am not the one suffering (but Peter was).

God does not meet Job on his own terms; he has not chosen either of the alternatives Job thoughtfully supplied to Him. He speaks past the dilemma presented to Him. Job and the friends had failed to see that for God simply to guarantee to people the proper result of his every action would be to reduce Himself to moral insignificance. He would never be free to act on his own. Such a God is helpless before either human vice or human virtue. A good bureaucrat could just as well work out the facts and assign what is due. Now people can live intelligently. They can figure out what they want and devise an algorithm for their life that will get it. All a just person wants from God is a guarantee that the system will work; otherwise, the scandalous possibility arises that a person may not get what is due them. If the system did work, then God would no longer have free will Himself. If one were to seriously consider the system of retribution, it may not seem so desirable after all. Everything could be preplanned and all actions tailored to a specific goal; there would be no surprises or spontaneity. People discover a kind of moral law operative in history and frequently become their own executioners. Those who sow hatred reap death. Any historian knows that frugal, moral, conscientious, and hardworking people are the world's best citizens and taxpayers.

All human experience rests upon the structure of cause and effect. We do the work our boss assigns because we expect to be paid. Just like with the retribution principle, we expect repercussions if the work is not done. The simplest of actions are done because one lives in confidence that expected results will follow. When they do not, most people can either discover what went wrong, so that the system is not jeopardized, or assume that something did go wrong, to the same effect.

Satan had suspected that Job served God only because of the predictable, dependable relationship between piety and prosperity. Give an animal two choices, and he will choose the better for him. A cat will always seek the warmest, softest place for his cat nap. Even my pet cockatoo has a cage with the top always open, yet he feels most secure on his familiar perch inside the cage. This is the role created things play; this is also the role Job wants permission to play. Just as a wild thing best attains its glory in the proper climate, people develop honor in the environment of health and wellbeing. The fence that kept Job perfectly safe was in reverse function a prison: the prison of inexorable process.

The Job who had kept his house in order and had been consistent in his piety could hardly be expected to serve God for nothing. There should be rewards for good behavior. So Job asks to go back to his well-functioning estate with the protective hedge Satan had noticed (1:10) of his good days, where a person could depend on God. All people look back to paradise in the past, and in so doing lose the present and sacrifice the future. But the entrance to paradise is not behind, but ahead. Job asks for a restoration of the old status quo. Being a moral person, he wants his honor.

In the first part of God's speech in chapters 38 and 39, He reminds Job of the differences between them. He reminds Job of his lack of knowledge and so he does not know what he is talking about. To illustrate, God asks Job a series of questions. This is often referred to as the 40 questions of Job. I counted them several times and came up with a different number each time; forty is a good biblical number, so I will go along with it. As we examine the questions in detail, we find a least three categories which will be elaborated below. At first Job is questioned about his role in creation and where he was when it took place. Implied is the fact that Job lacked the power to possibly do any of the acts of creation. These are questions that mortals cannot answer. The second category is of things that mortals don't know, but with their God-given intellect, they can find out. Answering these will require an effort; the answers are not given a priori. The set of questions that would be asked today would be different, but just as intriguing. The third set involves asking what humans can control. There may be some things in which humans have some semblance of control but not quite as complete as we imagine. There are some that never quite yield to our control and pose a threat. When it appears that one is yielding, another appears to replace it. Some of the threats may be natural and others are man-made. Ones of our own doing may ultimately be the most difficult to control. Underlying all of them is the fact that they present no problem to God.

The initial questions concern who it was, after all, who created all of this? It is interesting to compare this passage with Genesis 1. God was the one who created the universe:

> In the beginning when God created the heavens and the earth, the earth was a formless void and darkness covered the face of the deep, while a wind from God swept over the face of the waters. (Genesis 1:1–2)

Verse two shows that there was still a lot of work to be done before the earth would be ready to support life and, in particular, humanity. Job was not even around when this happened:

> Where were you when I laid the foundation of the earth? Tell me, if you have understanding. Who determined its measurements—surely you know! Or who stretched the line upon it? On what were its bases sunk, or who laid its cornerstone when the morning stars sang together and all the heavenly beings shouted for joy? (Job 38:4–7)

Similar parallels can be drawn to other aspects of creation: Genesis 1:9–10 to Job 38:8–11 and Genesis 1:14–15 to Job 38:12–15 and other allusions in Job 38. Thus chapter 38 is a retelling of the creation account. The message is phrased differently because the two accounts have different intended audiences and purposes. Genesis was to provide for the development of a nation from this people who had been slaves in a foreign land. They needed to be weaned away from the Egyptian culture and shown the falseness of their gods. Job was written to an individual (Job) to correct the defects in his (Job's) theology (and serve as a guide for others' theology). This may seem a cruel way to answer a person in Job's condition, yet we see what God is trying to convey and is showing that He is responsible for everything that exists, including Job himself; therefore should not Job recognize that if God deals properly with the events in our lives, then will He not also deal honorably with Job? The fact that God does not refer Job to the creation account written by Moses in Genesis probably means the Book of Job was composed prior to Moses's time. It is possible that the creation account existed in oral form before Moses actually wrote it down. In a similar way, the story of Job existed as an oral account before it was written down. There is simply a lot in the natural world God has created that humans do not yet understand. Verses 38:31–33 concern the stellar realm. The two constellations mentioned (Pleiades and Orion, which Job had referred to in 9:9) were worshiped by some as gods along with the Mazzaroth (the twelve constellations of the Zodiac). Even today people still check their daily Horoscope. In Job's time the physical laws governing the heavenly bodies were not known although some of their behavior was being cataloged and used in prediction their future movements. The causes of the rain cycle or the rain cycle itself was not understood as well as all the other atmospheric phenomena associated with it. Such knowledge was within the grasp of human intelligence, but it had to be recognized as God's creation and not gods themselves 38:34–38).

There was still much to be discovered in the wild animal kingdom as well. They were created perfectly capable of fending for themselves without human interference (38:39–39:18). Domesticated animals are not always completely under human control. Though used by humans, horses still exhibit their wild nature. Falconry accomplished much, but the birds of prey are basically free. There are more species today that are wild than have been domesticated. Asian elephants have long been used for work and interact very well with humans; the African elephant on the other hand has not been tamed; however, God does have the ability to completely control the wild beasts; this will be expanded in chapters 40 and 41 to include the mythical beast of chaos.

Many of the questions God asked of Job can be answered now. With just a few clicks on his smartphone with right apps, Job could have gotten answers for many of the questions, or he could just secretly ask Alexa or Siri. We have "stretched the line upon the earth" and know when "the mountain goats give birth."

Those questions are followed by who now is in control of creation? The question that must be asked of God's appearance is this: Is the voice from the whirlwind simply a noisy scolding which Job must endure before being restored to his lost estate? Is the status for which Job asks the ultimate one for humans? Or can God communicate to Job that there is an honor rooted not in affluence and fame but in constant human worth transcending circumstances?

There are those who think that the answer to Job was the confrontation itself. God is the answer in His mysterious power and presence. God's appearance in the story is like the scene from Shakespeare's *Romeo and Juliette* where Juliette is waiting for Romeo on her balcony and asks, "Wherefore art thou, Romeo?" And Romeo pops up out of the bushes and says: "I'm right here!" Job has been complaining all along that God is absent and wonders where He is; God pops out of the whirlwind and says, "I'm right here; and what's more, I have been here the whole time! All you really had to do was look around and you could see evidence of my presence. I'll give you a little quiz to illustrate." The friends had been talking about God; this is God (42:5–6). It is improbable that Job actually saw God in the cloud; what he doubtless means here is that he has perceived God in a new way—a real way. His knowledge of the Divine has been moved from rumor to experience. Of what does Job repent? Unable to see his sin because of the defects of his own perceptions, Job suddenly senses that he is inexcusably unclean. This not really a new revelation; Eliphaz had pointed it out from the start of the dialogue.

> Can mortals be righteous before God? Can human
> beings be pure before their Maker? (Job 4:17)

Job admits that this is true.

> Indeed I know that this is so; but how can a mortal
> be just before God? (Job 9:2)

Job does not repent of his pretrial days. He repents of what he has said during the trial (42:6).

God is somehow more than Job had expected. Job's questions are neither answered nor refuted; they are transcended. The question is, "What is this confrontation?" It is proper to seek in the enigmatic words of God a hint of His conception of the ultimate status of humans.

Is the distance between God and humans preserved? Something spoken can be misunderstood, argued with, or disobeyed. The forces and drives of the natural are beyond negotiation. We are still unable to precisely predict lightning, when and where it will strike, because invisible forces impel it. But only people may speak with God. Only humans are endowed with the capacity to miss God's meaning because we are humanly flawed and sometimes we need to be told. The apparent harshness of God's opening statement is in reality a compliment to Job. In being asked to respond to a question, Job is really being granted responsibility for himself.

It is indeed true that in all God's speech there is no reference to the tragedy of Job. The questions God asks relentlessly press the point of human ignorance and powerlessness (38:4, 12, 31). The whole phenomenal universe, in its creation and subsistence, is a mystery to Job. But he can consider it! Indeed that is part of the charge given to humans in Genesis 1:28 to "fill the earth and subdue it." Job can hear the questions, and because he can hear them he can pursue them! The questions of the voice of thunder are the questions of science. God does not forbid investigation. He does proclaim human ignorance; and it is assumed that whatever humans learn, there will still be "the beyond" that they do not know.

The author of Job would be amazed to know what people now have ascertained about the measurements of the earth (38:5) and delved into the other questions (38:16, 25, 35, 37). Modern science would appear to have taken the thunder out of the voice of the whirlwind. A second thought about God's speech should make it clear that he spoke, not in relation to ultimate problems, but from just ahead of the moving edge of human's learning. God has always chosen to reveal Himself to people in categories they could understand. The questions posed clearly testify to the rise of the scientific spirit. It is of interest that this new force was placed subsequent to Job's experience of new theological freedom. The finalities of dogma can shut off from the ears not only fresh news of God, but also new understandings of themselves and their surroundings.

A person standing silenced before the enlarged perimeter of their ignorance, confronting the more that they do not know, is not humiliated before heaven. They are honored with the status of coworker with God. It is significant that while God speaks of His care for all creation—inanimate, animate, and fabulous—He never speaks of His care for people. Perhaps this simply means that Job, already knowing how God cares for the rest of the world, is expected to discover for himself that providence extends to him too. Job knows that God cares for small things such as grass and baby ravens (38:27, 41; see Matt. 6:26–30). Should not such a God care for Job too? The problem is that the shadow of insecure tomorrows brings anxiety into the present. It is one problem to convince a chronic worrier that tomorrow's threats will never materialize; it is quite another to convince today's victim that he is not a victim. It would be possible for Job to have an answer without being told. The sufficiency of God, accepted through faith rather that experience, would be discovered and appropriated, rather than as instinctively received, without alternative, by animals.

Should Job find himself, in a sense, a creature of God, but as a creature whose own will and intelligence were necessary to complete the span of providential care, he would discover in humanity a dignity apart from all other life. Humans are not dealt with as creatures in God's speech. Were Job simply the creature of God, there would be no voice from the storm. That God comes and speaks to Job is in itself a guarantee to Job that he is a "somebody." His experience violates his idea of what life ought to be. But he does exist before God.

After the first half of God's speech (chapters 39–40), Job does not admit to sin, and he admits to presumption and that he is not on par with God.

> Then Job answered the LORD: "See, I am of small account; what shall I answer you? I lay my hand on my mouth. I have spoken once, and I will not answer; twice, but will proceed no further." (Job 40:3–5)

It will take another speech from the whirlwind, but at the end Job admits that he really did not know what he was talking about.

> Therefore I have uttered what I did not understand,
> things too wonderful for me, which I did not know.
> "Hear, and I will speak; I will question you, and you
> declare to me." I had heard of you by the hearing
> of the ear, but now my eye sees you. (Job 42:3b–5)

The clearest indication that God considers Job a responsible person rather than a defective creature is found in a brief interjection between the two main sections of the speech from the storm. Job's first reply is about his smallness (40:4–5). Dissatisfied with this noncommittal answer, God opens a second interview in which he challenges Job to justify his pretensions.

> Deck yourself with majesty and dignity; clothe
> yourself with glory and splendor. Pour out the
> overflowings of your anger, and look on all who are
> proud, and abase them. Look on all who are proud,
> and bring them low; tread down the wicked where
> they stand. Hide them all in the dust together; bind
> their faces in the world below. Then I will also
> acknowledge to you that your own right hand can
> give you victory. (Job 40:10–14)

The glory that God tells Job to deck himself with is, ironically, the glory proper to God. Job has attributed to God alone the capacity to humble all human greatness (12:13–25). At the same time, he has attributed all wisdom and might to God (12:13). God is here speaking to the whole human race, of which Job is representative; He is really speaking past Job to the audience who by now have identified themselves with him. People have been unable to fulfill his standards of justice in the freedom given them to form the structures of society. People suffer under tyranny and are exposed to genocide. Many people languish in poverty while others have more than they will ever be able to use. Who are they to accuse God of mismanagement of the universe? God, having made humans free, does not accept total responsibility for history.

Pride and self-sufficiency, rather than moral disorder, are the basic indictments which God places on society. It is humanity's false view of themselves that is the real disease. Job, whose integrity has sustained him through all his trials and whose final posture was to stand like a prince before God, has at last fallen into sin. His sin has not been the rejection of God prophesied by Satan, but rather Job's terms as he has dictated them to God.

If God and people operated only on the principle that each has their duty to perform and mutually desired results will ensue, there would be no force of history and creativity involved in human affairs. Job has not been receiving justice and he considers it God's place to provide it and asks Him to do so. But human experience may not so much fall short of justice as go beyond it. Too often people limit their awareness of justice to their own experiences. Under the impulse of terrible new forces, Job has already been compelled to explore realms otherwise undreamed of. Satan made it clear that only one as righteous as Job would be a suitable subject for his new experience. The response to his pain, the very depth of his outrage, has been conditioned by his former state. Only one who has risen high can plunge to profound depths. Only one who has known the thrill of belonging can savor the full bitterness of alienation.

When God refuses to accept the closed system of alternatives in the challenge Job presented, He implicitly gives Job the opportunity to accept a new role. Job can surrender without negotiation. He can accept God's way even if this means that the ashes of Uz remain his ultimate destiny. He can accept the right because it is right, even knowing the horror that might continue to attend it.

The new alternative emerging for Job is created by his trials. The issue on which the test began was whether a person was good because they found it to their profit or because of their unselfish devotion to the will of God. Through the medium of the debate, Job is forced to search for new meaning; his integrity remains intact, but there is a wider certainty, the justifying force of integrity in itself. There is a categorical right that transcends the immediate effects of human action and is grounded in God (31:13-15). As an example, Job is good to his slave not simply because he would be a better slave, but because God made them both the same way.

The pride that makes Job liable to the judgment of God and the pride that holds Job's world together are two sides of the same coin. With the withdrawal of the God of pious tradition, Job has in fact enthroned a new God to replace Him: the God of that which is right in itself. Job clings to God as He ought to be, but not to God. He wants God to be and to do the right as Job himself understands it. When the God of his traditional definition of justice fails (cause and effect), Job turns to the powerless, helpless "right in itself." Job gives his heart to a God who fails to manifest in history and experience inescapable credentials of divinity or majesty.

In his quest, Job does not lose God but loses the image of the God who is put to the test while Job is tested. Both have been found wanting; a new Job is now able to communicate with a new God. The rebel of Uz discovers God without knowing it. Satan's question is answered. He did not ask whether Job would remain theologically correct; he asked whether he would serve God for naught. The trial is not simply the assaying of gold nuggets already present, but becomes the crucible in which the gold is refined. The trials are Job's opportunity to know God somehow in himself.

It is possible theoretically to say that a human can never reject God when He appears as objective, proven majesty. (Even the devils believe and tremble. James 2:19). People are free to accept God without overt coercion. True, God may not appear therefore as the mightiest force in experience. To serve Him may not seem sensible. The acceptance of God may appear the least attractive, the least plausible, of all presented alternatives. But the unaccountable attraction of the right in itself continues to beckon, and in its weakness, may conquer us.

Job's difficulty is that the identity of his new God is based in himself. His conscience is the pillar and ground of the universe. Job needs to be freed from the half-truth of his new idolatry, so that he can sense the God who is beyond himself—the right that transcends definition.

> Will you even put me in the wrong? Will you
> condemn me that you may be justified? (Job 40:8)

God turns Job's eyes to a world outside himself that is oblivious to the importance of a mortal, resistant to their inquiries, and not susceptible to their management. God gives accounts of creatures that may not be tamed, a sea creature and a land creature (40:15–24 and 41:1–34). The creatures here are not necessarily known creatures. The Hebrew words are very rare. This occurrence of Behemoth is the only one in the Bible. (There are a few references in the contemporary literature such as the Apocrypha so the idea of such a mythical beast was known.) From the description of it and its behavior, many originally thought it might be an elephant but later assessment seemed more like a hippopotamus (but the tail is wrong). The description is not intended to provide information to visualize the beast, but to indicate its fearsomeness and strength. The Hebrew word translated Leviathan generally means "great water animal." Isaiah 27:1 calls it "the piercing serpent." Genesis 1:21 tells of God creating the "great sea monsters." Whether this is a precursor to Leviathan or simply indicating the large sea creatures, is open to question. The closest actual animal that fits the description of Leviathan is perhaps the crocodile, but not very close. Both of these creatures are African. Perhaps they have wandered close to Palestine or maybe tales of them have drifted up from lower in Africa making them even more mysterious. Both of these creatures could be mythological creatures who are the personification of threats and understood as such, much like the word "dragon" is used today. All that is important about them is that they represent a fearful threat and are untamable. While the most fearsome creatures today fall easy to humanity's modern weapons, the threat they posed has not vanished. (Actually 41:17–20 sounds more like a steam locomotive than anything else.) Instead we live under the threat of missiles, nuclear weapons, and terrorists (as was shown in the 9/11 attacks). Monsters symbolized the pathos of a mortal's inadequacy amid his surroundings. They continue to be spawned by new breakthroughs in technology and invention. Modern humanity is threatened more by the tiniest microbe (coronavirus, for example) than by the largest beast. Man has continually been confronted with the untamable.

People are liable to get the impression that there is something about this world that doesn't like them and will not submit to them. God may slap the rump of Leviathan and make a plaything of Behemoth, but he talks to humans. He holds them responsible. Job must be something of an alien in the universe to be a companion of God. To sink back into natural law and resume his creature like role is really to lose freedom, to lose self, to lose God.

A mortal is not to rest their hopes upon negotiating a system in which God and they act together in justice because, for mortals, there can be no justice. Human experience is so complex, so much the result of interacting forces beyond the control of humans, that no judge can assign to offenders what they precisely deserve for their crime. Similarly just rewards for virtue cannot be computed. Natural consequences will follow any action. Few claim that such consequences in themselves meet the demands of justice. "A tooth for tooth" is only superficially just. One tooth was broken out on impulse, the other in deliberation. One victim had no premonition that a tooth would be lost; the assailant had long moments of unhappy anticipation before the books were balanced. These experiences do not balance. Legal systems properly struggle to correct the deficiencies of natural law in order to create a workable discipline within society, but justice is a myth. When a person is punished, very frequently they so adjusts their moral universe so that the penalty is experienced as persecution. The executioner punishes. The victim however is not punished; they are martyred. Mostly today when people cry out for justice what they really mean is they want revenge. If we seriously think about it, most of us would rather not have true justice; we require mercy. We are probably better off not getting what we deserve. Zophar would probably be right; "He exacts of us less than our guilt deserves" (11:6b).

Actions still have consequences. One must accept responsibility for their actions. The consequences simply cannot be described satisfactorily as rewards or punishments. Experiences consequent to dishonorable actions may really appear to be desirable. Observers may be unable to discover any evidence of effective judgment in the aftermath of sin. This does not mean that there is no judgment, or that moral effects are unrelated to causes. It simply means that the consequences of man's deeds are frequently irreconcilable with any discernible system of punishments and rewards.

It is true that Job's acceptance of the will of God comes while he is under severe indictment for his mistaken judgments about God. No threats are made. He repents because he has seen God; his views are inconsistent with the God he now knows, so he abandons them. God's coming is neither reward nor punishment but a consequence of a mortal's creative outcries. God addresses the theology of the dialogue before Job's status is finally restored.

> After the LORD had spoken these words to Job, the LORD said to Eliphaz the Temanite: "My wrath is kindled against you and against your two friends; for you have not spoken of me what is right, as my servant Job has." (Job 42:7)

The three friends had presumed the role of God and passed judgments, offered terms, and suggested solutions when they were not fully informed of the situation. Job never denied that God had the right and the power to do what He wanted, but misinterpreted his trials for punishment that was undeserved and cried out at the miscarriage of justice.

That God comes to Job indicates something was right about what Job did. Job's stated conclusions are faulty largely because of self-centeredness and the inadequacy of inherited views to explain the terrible new world into which he had been flung. But his struggles toward God puts him in a new dimension of experience where he becomes able for the first time to come to terms with the inexcusable madness of his world without losing honor.

It is difficult for us to reconcile God's address to Job with the pleas that Job has offered. God is saying to Job that he has been worrying about the wrong things. To set the record straight, let's understand who has created all of this. Job did not do it, was not even involved in it, and didn't have the ability to do it.

Humans did not decide the measurements of the earth or determine the values of the constants of nature which have to be very finely tuned for life to exist. They may learn about these things, but they did not create them. Mortals may control very small portions of the seas but they did not determine their overall extent. Humans may have learned how to illuminate the earth, but they can do nothing to control natural day and night (daylight savings time doesn't really save anything). Furthermore humans have not done a very good job with the things they can do. Despots still reign, people are controlled by pride to succor their bruised egos, bigotry clouds minds, rioters irrationally rage, nations war with one another with detriment to their citizens, and evil people thrive. Is combating evil really only God's job, or do mortals have a responsibility in it? And now you propose to tell me how to run the universe?

However there are some things that mortals can do. They were created in the divine image, given agile minds, and ordered to fill and subdue the earth. They did not create the wild creatures, but they can study them and learn their habits. Animals can be trained to a certain extent, but ultimately their behavior is that endowed by God.

Therefore, Job, your concerns should not be about those you voiced, they should be about who is really in charge. Some writers have characterized the encounter between God and Job as God saying, "I'm God and you are not." Other writers have not liked this. Perhaps they are both right in the context in which they find themselves. However we need to see what God is saying about their relationship. God is saying, "I am not your bosom buddy, I am not your pal, I am not your BFF, I am not a friend, I am not a bookkeeper for dealing out rewards and punishments; some things you are responsible for, but you haven't done such a good job. I am your creator, your God, your king, your sovereign Lord; now show some respect." Nowhere in the Bible is God ever referred to as friend.

CHAPTER 12

Epilogue and Recovery

Love becomes the ultimate answer to the ultimate human question.
—Archibald MacLeish

S atan received an answer (1:21) to his question (1:9) in the prologue. Is the final pronouncement of the Job of the dialogue the same thing? The true nature of God was not revealed in the prologue. If He gives only to take away, if He bestows good only to counter balance evil, what is His true nature? What God has given for no reason He may repossess for no reason. The Job of the prose knows what God is doing, but then mortals are no different from any other part of creation.

Significantly, Satan did not claim that Job would deny the existence of God as a result of all of his catastrophes. Perhaps Satan knew enough about Job to know that that would never happen. All the way through the debate with the friends, Job never doubted that God existed; in fact, he suggests that God is the force behind all that is happening to him. That is why, when Job cannot reach reason with the friends, he directs his comments directly to God. When tragedy strikes, people today tend to deny that God exists. It is often phrased something like, "If God existed and is really good, He would not let such a thing happen." As mentioned earlier, one of the certainties that arises in the Book of Job is that the pious and innocent are not exempt from the natural laws established by God in creation even if it results in tragedy. Rather, faith comes from deeper within. The faith that God had in Job at the beginning is ascertained. Job has learned a truth about God; what He has given for no reason He can take away for no reason. Service and devotion to God are not for gaining materially, nor is the lack or destruction of material possessions a sign of God's displeasure. Job's fortunes are restored in the epilogue, not because God was required to do so by the retribution principle, but because He could and wanted to.

Job probably has a deeper appreciation for his material wealth at the end and has become cognizant of his obligations toward it. Herds and flocks require care and attention as do the servants who work for Job. At the back of his mind, amid all of the restored possessions, Job had to realize the transitory nature of them. They were taken away once, they could be so again. We noted earlier how this had actually been a fear of Job all along (3:24–26). He also learned that God's care and keeping were not passive assurance, but required Job's diligence for their completion. Just as God cares for the hawk (39:26–30) and the sparrow (Matthew 10:29–32) Job should know that He will care for him too; but it requires an active participation on Job's part. The provision has been made in the established natural laws in which both good and bad will happen. He may know the number of hairs on your head, but you still have to wash and comb it. And just as we may feel somewhat secure in the quantity of material possessions, we have to know they could be taken away as well. A pandemic could easily cause economic disaster and chaos, the stock market could crash, unemployment soar because employers are bankrupt, our pension funds be depleted in a very short time because of nothing we have done.

When Job recants at the end of the poetry, he proclaims a purpose of God which, though he cannot justify, he accepts. He has attempted to understand that which was beyond understanding. Because of his experience, something has happened; for the Job who had heard of God now sees Him, and is enabled by the ultimate vision to respond in an acceptance expressive not of the piety existing when the test began, but of a capacity produced by the test itself. The test has been a means by which the worth of a person may be not simply be assessed but created. God uses suffering, which seems to be the least expressive of the worth of humanity, as a mediation of humanity's ultimate worth. Job is permitted to explore the alternatives to resignation. His peace is not an extension of sublime, uninterrupted calm; it is the aftermath of an inner storm of which the revelatory whirlwind serves as a representation.

Job was attuned to meanings he could not have caught had he not been led to the gates of hell. That Job is able to accept God whom he cannot understand argues he has experienced faith. Because Job accepts God's unpredictable will, he cannot be accused of serving God calculatingly. Job's faith in God is not a mental projection of known consequences. It is a faith in God Himself.

Job's honor does not rest upon his estimate of himself. Knowing God through experience, Job's capacity to find worth in God Himself is the source of his honor. A person comes to God in freedom. To the extent that one accepts God, they become a self. The person who thinks only of himself is a person with no identity. Only those outside themselves can be real persons. Because Job considers integrity of greater value than self, it can overcome all selfish considerations. Through faith, honor becomes inward because faith is personal. It is more nearly a commitment than an acknowledgment.

The epilogue does not violate the rest of the book. First, God clearly insists in the prologue that Satan not take Job's life. Second, so far as Job is concerned, he has no intimation that he is going to be healed when he makes his recantation. Third, if God has to execute Job in order to assert the fallacies of the doctrine of moral retribution, He must submit to the grip of another closed system just as restrictive as before. God will have to be non-retributive. God can afflict Job, but He can also bless him without rewarding him.

Does the restoration at the end really make up for what was taken away at the beginning? What about the servants who were slain? Would having ten more children (was this a punishment for Job's wife?) really make up for the loss of the first ten?

There is no solution to the problem of Job. Elihu probably solves the problems of the dialogue best. The Book of Job should not be prescribed as a panacea for suffering. To know the Book of Job will not forestall anguish and despair, but it may direct the experience of tragedy toward faith. The reader will not expect pat, moralistic solutions to solve the brutal riddles which confront them. To get something from the book demands a response from the reader. God speaks to one as one is able and active to hear. The stationary reader hears nothing new from God.

Job required inward strength to survive. Faith bears the burden of committing the heart to certainties expressed in shaky human terms. The Book of Job insists that cherished ideas be liable to honest examination. Courage and struggle are necessary to accept truth in a changing world. Sometimes one is most faithful to the traditions of his forefathers when he discards or reshapes them. The demands of honor are never completely fulfilled. Honor is endangered not so much by those who violate their own codes as by falling into irrelevance. We are not so much in danger of tragedy as we are of becoming incapable of tragedy. The lack of individual honor is not our problem; it is the erosion of the tradition of honor that threatens us. The worst attacks upon the dignity of others are unconsciously delivered when we reveal that others do not exist for us. Effective honor is a force in itself.

The church inherits a peculiar responsibility. It must not allow itself to become nationalized, for it does not exist to serve the nation but exists to save souls. The honor we learned from the Book of Job demands honesty above conformity. The church must not assume the attitudes of Eliphaz, Bildad, and Zophar who too often captain the companies of the saved, drawn up in indomitable array before the dead god of Irreproachable Dogma. The church should learn to respect the mystery of God. It should not look to buildings, statistics, and community status for its identity. The Book of Job asks whether she can stand respectability.

Job could find solace neither in the traditional wisdom of the friends nor in the plausible philosophy of Elihu. His answer was not found in what God said and did, but in God Himself interpreted from the storm by the uncanonized revelations of agony and despair.

Is the question of Job ever really met? Jesus is in Himself a response to Job's outcry. Jesus did not yield to what seemed to be the demands of the times. He died because He was unwilling to sacrifice His integrity for safety and status in a lost society. The will of God was chosen, not because of the promise of the resurrection and ascension, but because it was God's will. Jesus did not confront God with alternatives. He saw that the alternatives were His own. He chose between self and God (this is what we should do at baptism).

A change in life occurs not simply because it is needed, but because one derives from the love of God an identity that begins to express itself in radical new decisions. Salvation always has to do with the quality of the self rather than with the rescue of self as an object. Being saved by going to heaven is analogous to seeking honor in the accumulation of things. The pleasures of heaven are not intended to repay present outrage.

Doctrines of Christianity that might be expected to answer the problem of Job are easily misused. The idea that suffering automatically ennobles is easy for the comfortable. It explains someone else's troubles and actually may produce the opposite effect. Catastrophes produce looters as well as heroes. Suffering ennobles only when it provides for a new expression for already-present honor.

The standards of Christian honor do not rest fundamentally on verbal codes. Love is not primarily emotional. It is the consistent assertion of the unconditioned and the incalculable worth of people. Christian righteousness is simply to act on the assumption that all people are as myself. The experience of God in worship and service begins to replace what had been sought in reputation and possessions. One who knows God does not need the reassurance of fame and fortune.

The extraordinary goodness and predicament of Job are not intended to place him outside human experience. They are to provide a setting where there is no question of the actual situation. Notice that Job was never informed that the events were a trial, nor how he fared during that trial. Thus it is clear that Job's faith was not "because of . . ." but "in spite of . . ." It is impossible to know the reasons for today's experiences.

The conclusions reached by the three friends concerning the reasons for Job's problems were the consensus of the wisdom of the times backed up by the interpolation of Elihu. Their consensus that suffering was evidence of sin was disputed by Job and in the end shattered by God. Consensus is agreement by the lowest common denominator. It implies there is no dissension while it actually suppresses it. No minority opinion is allowed. Everyone has to agree to some watered-down version of any decision. Only someone with the courage and integrity of Job can challenge conventional wisdom's assumptions. Notice that both Job and the friends stood by their convictions. The difference was that Job's were based on his inner strength (due to his superior knowledge of the facts) while those of the friends were based on the accepted doctrine of the day.

There are a number of practical lessons we can derive from the Book of Job for our lives. It is okay to argue with God because, rather than indicating a lack of faith, it exhibits a strong belief and acknowledgment of His concern and power. Two examples of others from the Old Testament are when Abraham pled for mercy concerning the destruction of Sodom and Gomorrah in Genesis 19, and when Moses pled for the Israelites after their sin of making the graven calf to worship while he was on Mt. Sinai in Exodus 32. In both cases God tolerated their arguing because they were devout and had a strong faith which did not waver. Their pleas were also for mercy for others.

Judging others requires more than observing external circumstances. This principle is so well known that it has become almost trite. Everyone knows the admonishment to walk in another's shoes before criticizing them, but most of us violate the idea with regularity. The tendency is to draw conclusions based on our own experiences and expectations while they almost never coincide with those of the other person. From Job we learn that a person's external condition may not reflect their internal world.

Attempts at comforting can have the opposite effect if empathy is absent. This is related to the previous paragraph; we offer solutions to the problems we perceive without digging deep enough to find the real ones. The sufferer may be reluctant to expose themselves for fear of being misunderstood. There is a whole catalog of ready-made answers that rarely fit the real situation. There is a sting to a solution that assumes the very opposite to one's behavior and attitudes.

In allotting the natural forces of this world, God does not necessarily distinguish between the righteous and the wicked. We all live in the same world subject to the same natural laws and forces; in the Bible they were violated in only a few very rare, very special circumstances. When the righteous and wicked are thrown together in close proximity it is impossible to maintain separation of phenomena. Pulling up the weeds can also result in pulling up the wheat (Matthew 13:24–30). Our concern is not only about this world.

Compare Job's final response (42:5–6) with his initial one (1:21; 2:10). Are they really the same thing? In the prologue God was an abstract concept evidenced by the felicity of Job's life until Satan intervened. In the epilogue God appears as a new reality in a more intimate way. The confrontation is no longer buffered by fulfilling mutual obligations. Now the communication is no longer through events that must be interpreted. Job has gained understanding apart from his status. How is Job's understanding at the end (42:2–3) related to his understanding at the start?

Does giving good counterbalance giving evil (2:10; Luke 12:48)? We often hear someone say "I'll make it up to you" when they have offended another. When we hurt someone through what we have said or something we have done, we attempt to reconcile it by saying such things as: "I didn't mean that the way it sounded" or "I take that back"; but this doesn't work. Because you can't take it back and remains forever a part of the relationship. You cannot go back and do it over again until you get it right. The only solution is to be forgiven. In a way isn't this what both Job and God are doing in the end?

There is no doubt that the Book of Job deals with a lot of suffering. Job had to endure the suffering brought on by Satan's tragedies; he also had to endure the suffering brought on by the ill-advised attempts by his friends to comfort him. Can suffering drive faith in either direction? Which is it for you?

Job receives double at the end; are the terms of the test violated? To answer that we have to ask, Did Job pass the test? His first response to the visit from the friends was to curse the day of his birth (3:1). Satan had predicted that Job would curse God to His face (1:11; 2:5), but Job's curse wasn't to God directly; it was only an expression of his anguish. Although Job consistently lays the source of his torments on God, he never condemns Him. Job can conceive of no other who has the power to bring about his agony (6:4). He does want to know why he is receiving what he considers to only be just punishment for the wicked. He has to face the problem the friends maintain that that is exactly what is happening. God had insisted that Satan spare Job's life; this indicates that He fully intended to restore Job's status if he passed the test. Thus the terms of the test were not violated because Job never knew why he was afflicted and that he would be restored if he persevered.

Where in the book is the solution to Job's problem(s)? The short answer is, nowhere. Even though God restores the fortunes of Job (42:10), things at the end are not exactly the way they were at the beginning. We don't know if there were any lasting physical effects such as scars, but there had to be psychological ones. You cannot suffer the loss of ten children and not be bothered. In spite of having ten more children, having lost everything once before, there must be anxiety that it could happen again. However Job has encountered God in entirely new ways and gained a great deal of understanding. He is better prepared to accept his life and better equipped to sympathize with others for their misfortunes.

Does the book provide a solution to suffering and will knowledge of the book forestall anguish and despair? That will depend upon the sufferer. There is no quick fix offered and no balm to ease the pain. One can only look to Job as an example of the course to follow. Be ready to let God know the depth of your despair (yes, He can already know it, but you need to express it yourself. 7:11). Never let faith waver or think that God does not hear or understand. One of Job's complaints was that God could not see things from a human perspective (9:32; 10:4–5). For Christians, we now know God has fully experienced the human condition through Christ (Hebrews 2:18).

Where did Job obtain the strength to survive the test? Spiritual strength is not something that can be conjured up on demand when needed. It is built upon true foundations from a life lived before God. It has to survive in spite of attacks from unlikely sources. The friend's consolations did not provide a framework on which to build. Without his integrity and honor, Job could have easily been discouraged and demoralized. Rather, he used the opportunity to reinforce and strengthen a spiritual stamina that had never been tested. He maintained his loyalty to God even as he felt he was being mistreated.

Are our ideas as rigid as Job's; are they liable to honest examination (1 Peter 3:15)? Often we may not remember the source of our ideas despite having a proof text which may or may not be applicable. After so long it is difficult to take a fresh look at our beliefs. But I believe the Book of Job is encouraging us to do so. The faith of our fathers really should be the faith of our own discovery.

There is no doubt that the teachings of Jesus speak to the problems of Job. He also set an example of how we should follow teachings we do not fully understand. The great advantage we have over Job is the assurance of an afterlife. Retribution is not the function of this life; it will be treated in the life to come. The problem still remains: do we serve God only for the hope of reward? In fact, is it proper for us in our prayers to ask favors of God? Can the pleasures of heaven repay one for present outrage? We will only know for sure when the time comes, but our faith should say "absolutely." But is happiness (or material things) inconsistent with Christianity? There have to be a lot of conditions to answer that and each person has to work it out.

The answer I see in the Book of Job is that it depends upon what their loss would do to one's faith and trust in God. And that depends very much upon the basis of one's Christianity. If we suffer circumstances that are as traumatic to us as Job's were to him, do we confront God with alternatives? What would make one repent or have a change of life? For most people, suffering can ennoble or embitter; the groundwork for which it will be has been developed throughout our lives. Salvation can be pursued to rescue self as an object, or it can be viewed as the opportunity to spend eternity with God. Would your integrity enable you to survive such a test as Job's?

Christians have a great advantage over Job; Jesus came and set the example for us. In him we see that God does understand human suffering and agony; Gethsemane showed us that. He did not have to die on the cross and ask that it be taken away, but only if it would be God's will. Why did Jesus chose to die on the cross? Was the resurrection the reward for His virtue? He had a commitment to keep that had implications far beyond Himself. All of humanity had a great stake in His actions. By them He asserted the worth of people, especially those who would follow Him. How does one assert the worth of people? To use the trite phrase from show business, "he is a tough act to follow." Difficulties arise when we try to do it all on our own. Job had only his past performance as an anchor.

Whether we have thought about it or not, we face a dilemma similar to Job's. What do you think your relationship to Jesus is? Do we worship only to gain from the relationship such as peace, calm, comfort, or help in time of need? Do we worship the Son to the exclusion of the Father? So much expression through the ages has been on the person of Jesus. Some want or claim to have a personal relationship with Jesus. But a very important thing happened in the fifty days from Jesus's crucifixion just before Passover to His resurrection on the day of Pentecost. During this time He went from being Jesus to becoming Christ. This was emphasized by Peter in his sermon to the multitudes.

> Men of Israel, hear these words: Jesus of Nazareth, a man attested to you by God with mighty works and wonders and signs which God did through him in your midst, as you yourselves know—this Jesus, delivered up according to the definite plan and foreknowledge of God, you crucified and killed by the hands lawless men. But God raised him up, having loosed the pangs of death for him, because it was not possible for him to be held by it. (Acts 2:22–24 RSV)

> Let all the house of Israel therefore know assuredly that God has made him both Lord and Christ, this Jesus whom you crucified. (Acts 2:36 RSV)

Jesus had worked hard to prepare the apostles for this event. Throughout His ministry He had difficulty shifting their thinking from an earthly perspective to a heavenly one. The passage in John 16 and 17 is a very significant discourse about the transition about to take place. It was difficult for the apostles to understand at the time; in fact, it was not fully appreciated until Pentecost. Indeed it is a difficult passage for us to fully comprehend. He told them that He was going away (John 16:5) and that His doing so was necessary for their benefit (John 16:7). Even so, there was the paradox that they would see Him no more and in a little while they would see Him (John 16:16), which greatly puzzled the apostles. This was true because His work on earth as Jesus was done (John 17:4) and He was being glorified as the Christ (John 17:5). Yet we tend to want to cling to His coat tails and say, "Don't go. Stay as Jesus." We want to keep Him in the manger, on the cross, or healing and comforting in the countryside rather than letting Him become the Christ.

This is the problem Job was having; he did not want to let go of the comfortable God of his former days and accept God as He is. God had to shake him out of his complacency recognize how the world worked and that he had a more significant role in it. Job, like us, is asked to give up his childish ways (1 Corinthians 13:11). Our knowing the Book of Job should draw us into a deeper relationship with God and acceptance of His ways.

Apparently there are those who think that when Jesus said in Matthew 20:28 and parallel passages that He came "not to be served but to serve" that they may call upon Him to do their every wish. We all know the context of the remark and that it is a call for us to serve others. In spite of what so many hymns, songs, and devotionals imply, as God emphasized to Job, there are a lot of things Jesus is not: He is not our bosom buddy, He is not our best friend, He is not our BFF, He is not someone we hang out with and pal around with. The passage in John 15:12–17 has sometimes been used to claim Jesus as friend; however, this passage is about love, sacrifice, and obedience, not friendship. John 15:14 specifically states that He consider one a friend if they obey Him. This is not what one would expect if He were only a pal or buddy. He is now our Lord, our Savior, our redeemer, our witness in heaven, our advocate with the Father. If one does a search through the New Testament, after the first five books, He is not spoken of as simply Jesus; it is always as Lord Jesus or Christ Jesus. These are titles given to indicate his status to us and ours to him. The Twelve and others called him "Teacher," "Master," or something similar. We don't know enough about royalty and its protocols in the US. In Britain the people do not call William their friend or pal; he is their prince. Our focus now should be on the Christ, not on Jesus. In the Book of Revelation he is referred to most often as simply the Lamb, but a very unique and important lamb. This does not take away any of the strength, comfort, and reliance that we have always had, but it should put it in proper perspective and ameliorate what our expectations are and our response to how those expectations are met. Ultimately our confrontation with God will be just as awe inspiring as Job's was. What will be the result (hint: Matthew 25:31–46)? What God has told Job, and also us, is, "I have not changed, I am still the same in my care for you. You can depend on things being orderly and predictable within limits. But you have to get the parameters right."

The Twelve constantly misunderstood Jesus and His mission; as Jesus, He was to prepare them for serving with the Christ (John 13:13). They had the concept of a coming king, but at the end still were thinking in human terms (Acts 1:6) after having already been given the heavenly perspective (Matthew 23:9–10). This was the message foremost in Paul's ministry (Philippians 2:9–11). The entire Book of Hebrews is concerned with our understanding of the Christ. In the New Testament, the church is never called "the church of Jesus." Most often it is simply the church or the church at____. It is called "the church of God" about seven times (Acts 20:28; 1 Corinthians 1:2; 11:22; 15:9; 2 Corinthians 1:1; Galatians 1:13; 1 Thessalonians 2:14), "the church of the living God" (1 Timothy 3:15), "God's church" (1 Timothy 3:5), "churches of Christ" (Romans 16:16), and "the church of the Lord" (Revelation 3:14). Paul leaves no doubt that the church is Christ's, for example, in Galatians and Ephesians, focusing now on the Christ instead of Jesus in no way diminishes His life or His work; rather, it enhances and exalts them. We now have the perfect example and guide to follow. We know God has had the opportunity to view things through human eyes.

In short God does understand the human condition; He does know our needs and wants. He has created us in His image and made us a coworker with Him. He has given us free will and expects us to use it and our intellect rather than relying on Him as the creatures do. This subjects us to both the ravages and blessings of natural forces; how we deal with them is up to us. Becoming rigid and unmoving stifles our ability cope with the results.

CHAPTER 13

The Power of
Negative Thinking

A man who lives, not by what he loves but what he hates, is a sick man.
—Archibald MacLeish

The popular conception of the Book of Job is that it is a study in patience and is a suitable source of comfort for those who are suffering. As we saw, this concept can only be conceived if one limits reading to chapters 1, 2, and 42. The difficulty in reading the remaining chapters causes many people to look merely at this portion of the book. Any careful study of the Book of Job leads to an entirely different perception. As pointed out at the beginning, different students come up with different thoughts because the book tells them different things. Even at different points in our lives, different concepts may emerge. This not to imply that any concept is wrong but that Job speaks differently to us based on our experiences and needs. Simply because one person may focus on a particular aspect does not mean that they reject others; rather, only that the current one is of interest at the time. Covering every aspect in a single volume would be impossible as evidenced by the large number of books written about Job. One can profit from reading many disparate viewpoints. This book is an attempt to focus on the negative thinking that is expressed by the characters and show how it shaped and directed the flow of the ideas.

As we see in the opening scene, a positive thought is often immediately counteracted by a negative thought. God's assessment of Job's righteousness and integrity evokes a negative comment from Satan. The power of that comment results in the test to which Job is subjected. Job's initial response is to the positive view of things (1:21). When God points that out to Satan, it only results in another negative comment from Satan. The power of Satan's second comment is such as to increase the intensity of Job's suffering. Job again endures and even rejects the negative comment from his wife (2:9). Job answers her with a little interruption in the domestic tranquility. Through it all Job refrains from sinning with his lips (2:10b).

All seems to be going well; Job is surviving the test and Satan is being proven wrong. Just when we think the problem has been resolved, a new factor enters the stage; three of Job's friends come to "condole and comfort" him (2:11–13). Therefore it comes as a shock when Job expresses his first negative thought. There is no indication as to what exactly triggered this response from Job other than that the three friends have been sitting with him for a week without saying anything. We are never told if anyone offered any credible physical aid to ease his suffering. Perhaps this is why Job wants them to know how desperate his plight really is. In graphic detail Job wishes that he had never been born.

> Let the day perish in which I was born, and the night
> that said, "A man-child is conceived." (Job 3:2)

Later in chapter three and again in chapter ten, Job repeats the thought a couple of more times (3:11; 10:18). But because his birth cannot be undone, he sees the only alternative is to be taken in death. He wonders why those who are in such misery are not released through death. Never at any time does he express the thought of taking his own life; that is God's choice and in His power to do.

> Why is light given to one in misery, and life to the
> bitter in soul, who long for death, but it does not
> come. (Job 3:20)

> O that I might have my request, and that God would
> grant my desire; that it would please God to crush
> me, that he would let loose his hand and cut me off!
> (Job 6:8–9)

His pain and torment are so severe that he loathes his life.
This gives him the right to express his complaints which he does
throughout the debate; first to the friends, and finally, directly
to God. The thought is introduced in his rebuttal to Eliphaz.

> I loathe my life; I would not live forever. (Job 7:16)

He repeats this in his next speech to Bildad (9:21; 10:1).

Negativism plagues him at various times through the rest of
the book interspersed with a few bright moments. Job has no
doubts about where his troubles come from; only one source
has that much power.

> For the arrows of the Almighty are in me; my spirit
> drinks their poison, the terrors of God are arrayed
> against me. (Job 6:4)

> Who among all these does not know that the hand
> of the Lord has done this? (Job 12:9)

> Know then that God has put me in the wrong, and
> closed his net around me. (Job 19:6)

Recognizing the source only adds to his misery because he
cannot contend with God. In fact, he does not even understand
why God would bother with him. If a confrontation is arranged,
Job is at a serious disadvantage.

> What are human beings, that you make so much
> of them, that you set your mind on them, visit

them every morning, test them every moment? (Job 7:17–18)

But how can a mortal be just before God? If one wished to contend with him, one could not answer him once in a thousand. (Job 9:2b–3)

Though I am innocent, I cannot answer him; I must appeal for mercy to my accuser. (Job 9:15)

If things continue as they are now, then Job has no hope and no future.

Remember that my life is a breath; my eye will never again see good. (Job 7:7)

Because Job is so sure the root of is troubles is from God, he wants to confront Him to find out why and argue his innocence before him. He comes to the realization that if he were to die, he would never have his name cleared; he must live to defend himself. Job is convinced if he has a fair hearing, he will be vindicated and restored to his pretrial state.

Teach me, and I will be silent; make me understand how I have gone wrong. (Job 6:24)

As he continues this theme his arguments become stronger and he becomes more confident. He expects God to be fair and deal out justice as Job himself understands it. His case is well prepared but that won't do any good unless he can get a hearing (13:3, 18; 19:23; 23:3–4). In his oath of clearance, he summarizes his contention and confidently outlines how he sees things will go.

O that I had one to hear me! (Here is my signature! Let the Almighty answer me!) O, that I had the indictment written by my adversary! Surely I would carry it on my shoulder; I would bind it on me like a crown; I would give him an account of all my steps; like a prince I would approach him. (Job 31:35–37)

Even as Job expresses his confidence in the solidarity of his case, he recognizes that he is really no match for his accuser. His mood swings from hope to utter despair. God's power is evident in creation and in His control of it (9:4–12), and no one can question His actions. His strength puts Him beyond any serious challenge from mortals; He cannot be subpoenaed to answer for His actions (9:19). Furthermore His mind is already made up and it cannot be changed so nothing but terror awaits Job (23:13–17). Job is very negative in his belief that God cannot understand the human perspective.

> For he is not a mortal, as I am, that I might answer
> him, that we should come to trial together. (Job 9:32)

Because of the inequity of power, Job needs someone to plead his case. Eliphaz has already implied that the three friends will not be taking up Job's cause because he doesn't have anyone to turn to.

> Call now; is there anyone who will answer you? To
> which of the holy ones will you turn? (Job 5:1)

This does not cause Job to give up hope although he probably expected more loyalty from his friends. Their negativity does give him an idea; there should, indeed there must be, someone to take his case. This thought leads to brief moments of hope which quickly dissipate because he does not actually believe such an advocate exists. His case can be strengthened stating the need. At first he realizes an important lack in trying to obtain justice from God.

> There is no umpire between us, who might lay his
> hand on us both. (Job 9:33)

Because of the lack of a mediator, Job is driven to propose what ought to be. He has no evidence for what he is stating but the demands of justice require something extraordinary. The fact that no help exists strengthens his case and implies that help should exist.

> Even now, in fact, my witness is in heaven, and he
> that vouches for me is on high. (Job 16:19)

> For I know that my Redeemer lives, and that at the
> last he will stand upon the earth; and after my skin
> has been thus destroyed, then in my flesh I shall see
> God, whom I shall see on my side. (Job 19:25–27)

Job's mood takes diverse forms driven by the impact of the friends words. Their approach is to refer to the retribution principle that what one is experiencing is exactly what one deserves based on their behavior. Naturally Job's condition is obvious evidence of unrighteous behavior. The first recorded speech from the friends is by Eliphaz in chapters 4 and 5 where he sets the pattern for the subsequent attacks upon Job. Any show of sympathy or recognition of Job's virtues is short lived. At first they describe, in general terms, what those who are wicked should expect to experience in their lives; the expectation is remarkably close to what Job is experiencing. Eliphaz observes:

> As I have seen, those who plow iniquity and sow
> trouble reap the same. (Job 4:8)

Bildad notes:

> See, God will not reject a blameless person, nor take
> the hand of evildoers. (Job 8:20)

Zophar gets more to the point:

> Know then that God exacts of you less than your
> guilt deserves. (Job 11:6b)

> For he knows those who are worthless; when he sees
> iniquity, will he not consider it? (Job 11:11)

As the dialogue continues, the accusations against Job become stronger, more pointed, and, of course, untrue. In each instance Job rebuts the speaker, rather forcefully at times. The effect on someone being subjected to such harsh accusations could cause them to lose self-esteem. Instead of the charges causing Job to recant and submit to humility, he grows more determined and confident. Job seems not to get the subtle message they are sending to him so they resort to general sins attributed to Job. Bildad shows the effect of his sins:

> Their strong steps are shortened, and their own schemes throw them down. For they are thrust into a net by their own feet, and they walk into a pitfall. (Job 18:7–8)

When this doesn't work either they name specific sins. Eliphaz sums up the problem:

> Is not your wickedness great? There is no end to your iniquities. (Job 22: 5)

These are but a sample of how the arguments go throughout the dialogue in chapters 4 to 27; all with a very negative view of Job's behavior. So as not to seem altogether too negative, they offer a solution in the form of behavior change which will doubtlessly lead Job's restoration. Thus Eliphaz is confident:

> How happy is the one whom God reproves; therefore do not despise the discipline of the Almighty. For he wounds, but he binds up; he strikes, but his hands heal. (Job 5:17–18)

Bildad is likewise sure that there can be a happy ending:

> See, God will not reject a blameless person, nor take the hand of evildoers. He will yet fill your mouth with laughter, and your lips with shouts of joy. (Job 8:20–2)

Zophar agrees:

> If you direct your heart rightly, you will stretch out your hands toward him. If iniquity is in your hand,

> put it far away, and do not let wickedness reside in
> your tents. (Job 11:13–14)

Such advice is contained at the end of all the three friend's speeches except chapter 25. It is summarized by Eliphaz at the end of his last speech (22:21–30) which begins with:

> Agree with God, and be at peace; in this way good
> will come to you. (Job 22:21)

This particular passage would serve well as an invitation to respond at the end of many a sermon; the only thing wrong with it is that it does not apply in Job's case. The reason a hearer of such an invitation does not respond is probably, in their own minds, they feel much like Job did; they have done no great wrong.

The friends are careful to cite the authority by which they make their judgments. Eliphaz at first attributes his to a vision (4:12–21), Bildad appeals to the teachings of the fathers (8:8–10), and Zophar is only saying what God would if he were to speak to Job (11:5–6). In his second speech (most of chapter 15) Eliphaz leaves no doubt but what they are speaking for God:

> The gray-haired and the aged are on our side, those
> older than your father. Are the consolations of God
> too small for you, or the word that deals gently with
> you? (Job 15:11)

Zophar has been informed by a spirit (20:2–3).

Job will have none on this; he does not believe they are truly speaking for God:

> Will you speak falsely for God, and speak deceitfully
> for him? (Job 13:7)

Because the friends have offered no real solution or comfort, Job describes their negative impact. From the very onset of the debate, the tension between Job and his friends is apparent. The friends are sure that Job has done something wrong and God is chastising him for; he needs to repent and turn back to God as Eliphaz had expounded in his first speech (5:17ff). To Job such pronouncements are an indication that he has been abandoned by them (6:14–27). As the debate progresses, the friends become more personal in their attacks and more pointed in their accusations. In return Job becomes very specific in the failure of the friends to comfort him; they don't even show sympathy.

The negative opinion Job has of the friend's attempts at help can be traced through the dialogue by looking at several passages. They terrify him with visions (7:13–14); they are smug in their conceit (12:2–3); their cures are worthless (13:2–5) because he is not inferior to them; they don't really speak for God (13:7–12); they are doing a miserable job of comforting him (16:2–5); their minds are closed (17:4); they continually attack him (17:10); they torment him (19:2–3); his friends have failed him (19:14); he is repulsive to his wife (19:17); his intimate friends abhor him (19:19); no matter what his defense the friends continue to mock him (21:2–3) as they scheme to wrong him (21:27); sarcastically he describes their help (26:2–4). In spite of such treatment Job will not back down and admit to falsehood (27:2–6). After reading these passages, one wonders how the debate remained as civil as it did and why did they continue? Apparently the friends did consider leaving early on in the debate (6:29).

The response to the climate on negativity prevalent throughout the Book of Job could and did take many forms. In all of them we see the power exerted by the negative thinking. Satan's negative opinion of Job's motives prompted God to allow them to be tested. Job's negative evaluation of the friend's ability to comfort him caused them to cease their attempts (32:1, 3). Rather than being discouraged and losing self-esteem, Job seems to thrive, and grows stronger as the debate proceeds. Job's negative declaration of God's running of the world caused God to answer him although not in the way Job expected.

There is undoubtedly a lesson here for us all when confronted with negative thinking. We can accept the challenge as God did with Satan and prove the thinking wrong. We can be disheartened, embittered, and feel like giving up. Yet this attitude will provide no solace, may reinforce the negativism, and have long lasting unwanted effects. We can use it as a stimulus to evaluate our own thinking from which we can build strength as Job did. Job survived because he had the inner strength and integrity to begin with.

Satan's mistake in assessing humans was assuming they were only interested in tangible things. Thus he was sure that the loss of material possessions would turn Job against God. When that didn't work then surely the loss of family would do the trick. He was wrong again. If loss of external things didn't have the power, then personal pain and suffering might work. Job showed that human beings are more than what meets the eye. Being made in the image of God endowed humans with an intangible something that defies observation. It is something that cannot be measured and assigned a worth like sheep and donkeys. Before the test Job himself was not aware of the depths of his self and strength that had never been exercised. The friends expressed that Job's troubles were the results of grievous misconduct rather than seeing if the cause really existed. First appearances caused them to assume that Job's negative behavior was the root of the evil he was experiencing. They relied on the prevailing wisdom of the masses that allowed no exceptions. The platitudes believed to have worked in the past proved to be inadequate when confronted with an anomaly. Empathy is hard to come by when rigid rules and convictions get in the way. Their minds were made up and they didn't want to let facts get in the way. But their biggest mistake was they felt that they were speaking for God.

Job's mistake was that he, like the friends, believed that he was in control of his world. He knew how the system worked and he played by the rules. For the system to not work required a power that was great enough to ignore the rules. He became negative, not only of the depth of commitment of the friends, but of the concern of the God whom he had always trusted. Reflecting on the past he became aware of injustice done to others before him; he was not alone. Sometimes the righteous suffered and the wicked prospered. Absolute justice was an illusion. In the system he had embraced there was no court of appeals, no way to right injustice. He believed God could be wrong when assessed from the human standpoint and that that was the one that mattered.

Elihu was wrong in believing the problem was that a message being sent was not received. It still required a correlation between cause and effect. He still held the opinion of the other three that catastrophe was evidence of sin. If a message was being sent, Job must have needed it.

God's message to Job, and likewise to the others, was that the reason for events cannot always be known because humans are not really in control of much. There are things that are unpredictable and uncontrollable. There are things that are just outside human knowledge that once they are revealed only expose further unknowns. Chaos persists in spite of the best human efforts. It is only recently that humanity has learned that very small causes can have major impact on later events; that there is a limit to the certainty with which things can be known; and that the action of observing can disrupt what is being observed. Although derived from the physical world, the importance to the nonphysical has become apparent.

The Book of Job should give us pause to evaluate our own relationship and attitude toward God. To do so we have to ask disturbing questions of ourselves. Why do we worship God, or put another way, what do we worship God for? Is it as Satan suggested, only for what we can get out of Him? What is the main focus and purpose of our prayers? What is the goal of religious devotion? Do our prayers become a laundry list of things we want from God or want Him to do? Actually as I read elsewhere in the Bible, the content of the prayers is not as important as the content of the individual offering them. First things must come first.

We have to resist making God in our image. He has assigned humans the task of subduing the world and He is not to be the muscle enforcing the moral order we have established. True, the moral order must come from and be based on the precepts He has revealed to us.

References

1. Carstensen, Roger N. *Job Defense of Honor*. Abingdon Press: New York and Nashville, 1963.
2. Morgan, G. Campbell. *The Answers of Jesus to Job*. Marshall, Morgan & Scott: London, 1950.   Republished, Baker Publishing Group: Grand Rapids, MI, 1973.
3. Safire, William. *The First Dissident*. Random House: New York, 1992.
4. Walton, John H. with Kelly Lemon Vizcaino. *The NIV Application Commentary, Job*.   Zondervan: Grand Rapids, MI, 2012.
5. Young, Robert. *Young's Analytical Concordance to the Bible*, 22 ed. Eerdmans: Grand Rapids, Michigan, 1964, 1969, 1970. Reprinted 1975.

Numerous Christian publishers have commentary series that include a volume on Job.

References 2 and 4 have extensive bibliographies on Job. You may also use the search capability on the internet to obtain other valuable reading material for further study.

ORDER INFORMATION

RELIANT
PUBLISHING
A DIVISION OF REDEMPTION PRESS

To order additional copies of this book, please visit
www.redemption-press.com.
Also available on Amazon.com and BarnesandNoble.com
Or by calling toll free 1-844-2REDEEM.

CPSIA information can be obtained
at www.ICGtesting.com
Printed in the USA
FSHW011733131221
86889FS

9 781646 453030